WALKING LONDON'S WATERWAYS

WALKING LONDON'S WATERWAYS

UPDATED EDITION

GILLY CAMERON-COOPER

IMM lifestyle books™

Read. Learn. Do What You Love.

Front cover image (top): © Nikada/istockphoto.com
Front cover image (bottom): © Willbrasil21/istockphoto.com
Spine image: Peter the Great with dwarf statue, Greenwich © Phil Kay
Back cover image: © StazioneCentrale/istockphoto.com
Photographs on pages 2, 11, 19, 23, 32, 39, 47, 54, 66, 73, 77, 94, 103, 115, 119, 127, 131, 139, 148, 157, 165, 173: © Gilly Cameron-Cooper
Photograph on page 85: © BreatheFitness/istockphoto.com

Published 2016—IMM Lifestyle Books
www.IMMLifestyleBooks.com

IMM Lifestyle Books are distributed in the UK by Grantham Book Service, Trent Road, Grantham, Lincolnshire, NG31 7XQ.

In North America, IMM Lifestyle Books are distributed by Fox Chapel Publishing, 1970 Broad Street, East Petersburg, PA 17520, www.FoxChapelPublishing.com.

ISBN 978-1-5048-0055-6

Printed in the United States of America

10 9 8 7 6 5 4 3 2 1

CONTENTS

The Ebb and Flow of London's History

I thought I knew London well; I have cycled from many a suburb to the centre, clawed my way around it by car and written many a city walk. Nevertheless, my ideal of exploring places on foot has generally been among the sculpted mountains, luscious valleys and dazzling shores of the Greek island where I run www.walkingplus.co.uk with my husband. Nothing could be more dramatically different than the industrial and urban landscapes of London's docklands and waterways. A poor alternative, you might think, but no, London's waterways offer exciting, rewarding and ever-changing territory, rich in history, discovery and even opportunities for some wildlife watching. You deepen your knowledge and understanding of one of the world's greatest capital cities, reaching parts you never knew existed – and most of these paths are passable for walking at any time of the year, and are also great routes for running and cycling. I hope that exploring the docks, rivers and canals will reveal for you, as it did for me, new perspectives, less familiar scenes and an insight into London's industrial history.

Breathing Space

Looking at London from the perspective of its waterways presents a different world, another level of existence away from the familiar sprawl of streets and arterial roads, shops, houses and offices. Ribbons of almost-rural green wind through unseen industrial and urban wastelands, concealed from view by graceful willows and poplars. Here, sheltered from the roar of traffic and the pace of city life, kingfishers dart, herons stand and wild flowers flourish. You may find yourself strolling beside a green-fringed canal, brown carp loitering just beneath the water's surface and gaily painted narrowboats sliding by, then catch the name of a familiar road on a bridge and marvel at the times you used that road in complete ignorance of the hidden world that lay beneath. In unexpected places, such as Woolwich, Bermondsey or London's old East End, you will discover a watery cut or basin lined with plane trees and pebbled paths, and occasional gems of modern landscaping that evoke the byways of Amsterdam.

Peeling Back the Past

London's docks, rivers and canals offer far more than welcome breathing space in a capital city. They are soaked in layers of history. The very life and development of London as a port, commercial centre and cultural capital evolved and revolved around its location on the River Thames, and the city's rises and falls in fortune are reflected in the stories its waterways have to tell.

Sometimes, you may feel that the docks and canals of today, bereft of the jobs for which they were created, are sterile and lifeless compared with, for example, 150 years ago, when they were vital links in the global trade of a thriving industrial nation. However, anyone walking along a waterway of that time would probably have been overwhelmed by the stench and detritus of industrial and urban pollution. Today, thanks to the efforts of organizations such as the Canal & River Trust (formerly British Waterways), enlightened local councils and conservation groups, pedestrians not only have unprecedented access to waterside paths, but can see aquatic plants and fish in the relatively clean water and breathe relatively fresh air.

It is their history, however, that makes these waterways particularly interesting to walk along, and the more you learn, the more you are able to look at a building or a scene and peel back the layers of its past. As you stand on the embankment of the River Thames at Blackfriars or Bermondsey you can imagine the broad tidal river that greeted Roman invaders in the 1st century AD: the river was sluggish between its silted shores and flanked by wastes of low-lying marshland dotted with tribal settlements, with the dense woodland of the Great Middlesex Forest beyond. You can mentally substitute the high-rises of new Docklands for Georgian docks packed with a bristling forest of masts, and the suburbs of Brentford and Wembley for the market gardens, which, at the beginning of the 19th century, dominated the countryside within 5–10 miles (8–16km) of the city, providing fruit, vegetables, meat and dairy products for the ever-growing population.

Exploring the city's waterways is to reach the heart of London's history. Stone Age people may have settled on the hillocks we now know as Ludgate (see page 151, *Bridging the Thames* walk) and Cornhill, protected by the Thames to the south and marshlands to the north and well watered by springs and streams such as the long-lost Walbrook and Fleet rivers. Soon after the Romans had established their control of Britain in the 1st century AD, Londinium, as they were to call the new settlement, became the obvious choice for a commercial and administrative centre. Gravel that had washed down to the mudflats by floods had formed shallows, which could be forded or bridged, and beaches, which provided firm ground for landing. The river became an increasingly busy trading route, carrying supplies to and from the rest of the Roman Empire, and the port of Londinium grew in importance.

Ships could sail up the Thames estuary and ride the high tide along the river, spreading the influence of invaders, such as the Vikings and French, on Britain's lifestyle and language far inland. These invaders also introduced exotic products and new trade, establishing London as the port and commercial centre that would eventually dominate the world. You will pass inlets where the Romans traded in wine and corn and the shores where our Saxon ancestors loaded bales of woven cloth to be shipped to the weavers of the Low Countries. You will gaze over reaches of the Thames from which adventurers set forth to find new trade routes in the age of exploration and walk along waterways that were once the pulsing arteries of communication in Britain. The piers, wharves, bridges and waterside buildings of the distant past have long crumbled or been covered by layers of silt and buildings. But the foundations of modern industrial England are still very much in evidence along the routes covered by this book.

Proximity to the sea meant that the lower reaches of the Thames and Lea rivers were tidal, a force that was harnessed to power tidal mills. The energy of tributaries flowing into the Thames, such as the Wandle and the Ravensbourne rivers, was also utilized: to power mills for grinding corn, gunpowder or snuff, or to drive machines that whittled water conduits from tree trunks or sharpened metal into sewing needles. The combination of its local resources, proximity to northern Europe and Thames-side location put London ahead of rival ports, such as Bristol and Portsmouth, making it Britain's capital and principal port, the focal point of both global and national trade and communications. The engineering feats of the Georgians and Victorians – which included an ambitious network of canals, massive dock-building programmes, bridges, viaducts, locks and steam engines – put Britain at the forefront of the modern industrial world, in which London played a pivotal role.

Exploring London's waterways provides an evocative insight into the extraordinary changes and achievements of the Industrial Revolution particularly, but also into Britain's pioneering marine technology, impressive achievements in trading and exploration, and social history through the ages. Because of their active contribution to the life of London – and Britain – the landscapes bordering the waterways have been prone to extraordinary upheavals and facelifts, of changing trades and industries, fortunes and populations throughout history.

London's Lost Rivers

There were victims of London's success story. Many of the rivers and millstreams that once provided clear spring water – at Clerkenwell, for example – were lost. As the city grew, marshland was drained and rivers were redirected and tamed by dams and sluices, banished to underground conduits and relegated to carrying sewage. Their courses were bricked over and, through the centuries, became hidden beneath successive layers of buildings, rubbish and road and rail routes. You may have been able to enjoy their bucolic attractions in the 11th century, but now the lost rivers are only remembered in the names of streets and suburbs, such as Holborn (meaning stream in the hollow), Fleet Street, Marshgate, Stratford and Knightsbridge, which is on the course of the Westbourne.

This book investigates the surviving rivers, such as the Wandle, the Brent and the Lea, which still offer waterside walks of great interest and some rural relief in an urban area. It is a different, but challenging experience to trace, via the pavements of central London, the courses of the lost rivers. A name plate on the Thames Path near Cannon Street Station recalls the one-time emergence of the Walbrook there (though the historian John Stow records that the small river was covered with buildings as long ago as 1598). The Fleet, once one of the largest of the Thames tributaries, degenerated into a brook that was frequently choked with rubbish, industrial effluent, raw sewage and dead animals. The Fleet was made into a canal after the Great Fire of London and then bricked over. Its present-day role is as a storm sewer emptying into the Thames at Blackfriars Bridge. The Serpentine lake in Hyde Park lies in the valley once fed by the Westbourne: the river itself is transported in underground pipes, which can be seen at Sloane Square Underground Station and emptying into the Thames at Chelsea. Pipes carrying the waters of the Tyburn pass through Victoria and Baker Street underground stations.

Exploring the Waterways

This book aims to give a sense of the history that shaped and was shaped by the waterways that you can still see, whether they be natural or manmade. I skim over many 'sights' en route – along the Thames especially – that owe little to waterside history and are well covered in more general walking books.

Most Thames-side and canal-side routes are all-weather gravel or better, but some riverside paths can be extremely muddy. Some words of warning: a few routes go through rundown areas, where you may feel safer walking with a friend or a dog. Direction signs on the route may not be reliable as it is a popular sport to rotate the signs upon their posts, and others may be obscured by graffiti. Directions found on websites tend to lack detail and consistency.

An urban landscape is forever changing. Construction and development for the 2012 Olympic Games had an enormous impact: in the book's last edition, many parts of the Thames near Greenwich and of the Lea Valley were closed. Now, both areas are enjoying regeneration. Waterways that trickled, heavy with pollution, through lost urban wastelands now flow strongly and cleanly. The Olympic Park has become Queen Elizabeth Park, a wonderful mix of leisure facilities, wild gardens and wetlands. The route between Greenwich and Woolwich, once blockaded by building sites, now hugs the river almost all the way, much of it along a wide boulevard dotted with works of art and planting schemes that are in keeping with the tidal estuary environment.

There will always be diversions around works in progress and new projects. But with readers' help, we plan to keep abreast of any changes. Just as you periodically update the software on computing devices, you will be able to keep in touch with the latest information on London's waterway routes by visiting and contributing to the blog at www.gillycameroncooper.com/walkinglondonswaterways. Send in your photographs, too. The site's success is dependent on reader interaction, so if you come across a change or improvement, a section of a route or towpath that has suddenly re-opened – or closed – post it!

I hope that using this book will give you as much pleasure as I had in researching and writing it.

Gilly Cameron-Cooper

KEEP UPDATED! Post your photos,
comments and any changes to the routes at:
www.gillycameroncooper.com/walkinglondonswaterways

KEY TO MAPS

Each of the walks is accompanied by a map in which the route is shown in blue. Places of interest along the walk, such as historic buildings and open spaces, are clearly identified, as are all underground and railway stations along the routes.

The following is a key to the symbols used on the maps:

KEY	
route of walk	public toilets
railway line	park
Docklands Light Railway station	lock
tramway	underground station
path	airport
major building	railway station
church	

Opposite: *Who would think that this luxuriant stretch of the River Lea is in the East London suburb of Hackney. The pink flower in the bottom left corner of the photo is the attractive but strong-smelling and invasive Himalayan Balsam.*

Walking London's Docks, Rivers and Canals

High Barnet

BARNET

Dollis Brook

Rural Brooks p144

Folly Brook

RICKMANSWORTH

Northwood

EDGWARE

FINCHLEY

Harefield

HENDON

HARROW

Hampstead

RUISLIP

WEMBLEY

Kilburn

UXBRIDGE

Grand Union Canal

Hay & Bricks p14

Greenford

Ribbon of Green p125

A Flight of Locks p20

Hanwell

EALING

Bridging the Thames p151

Grand Union Canal

West Drayton

M4

River Brent

Hammersmith

Sporting Thames p161

River Thames

HOUNSLOW

Barnes

Fulham

Thameside Retreats p170

Putney

RICHMOND

Twickenham

STAINES

WIMBLEDON

KINGSTON UPON THAMES

Thorpe

SUNBURY

SURBITON

CHERTSEY

WALTON-ON- THAMES

N

WEYBRIDGE

EWELL

Regency Waterway p44

The Lea's Marshy Origins p138

River Lea Navigation

Barges Go West p38

Old Rivers for New p130

Islington

Hackney

Shortcuts to Limehouse p28

Regent's Canal

Hertford Union Canal

Bow Creek

Georgian Dock Boom p51

Surrey Side Up p82

Limehouse Cut

Reinventing the Landscape p90

Wharves & Warehouses p100

Bulk Cargo p69

Royal Favourites p75

Georgian Docks Revisited p62

The Working Wandle p111

River Wandle

Country Wandle p118

ENFIELD
LOUGHTON
East Barnet
CHINGFORD
CHIGWELL
Edmonton
Tottenham
ROMFORD
Walthamstow
Hackney
DAGENHAM
Camden Town
Hackney
Barking
Marylebone
City
Stepney
East Ham
River Thames
River Thames
Lambeth
Thamesmead
Chelsea
Bermondsey
Woolwich
Deptford
Clapham
Brixton
Greenwich
Lewisham
BEXLEY
Dulwich
Streatham
Beckenham
BROMLEY
SWANLEY
CROYDON
ORPINGTON
SUTTON

0 1 2 3 4 5 km

0 1 2 3 miles

HAY AND BRICKS: GRAND UNION CANAL, HORSENDEN HILL AREA

Summary: We explore the Paddington Arm of the Grand Junction (later Grand Union) Canal along its most rural and leafy stretch, learning on the way about narrowboats and their cargoes. To the west, the Paddington Arm continues rather more grubbily through densely populated Greenford and Southall to Bull's Bridge junction, where it joins the main canal, but our route takes us up Horsenden Hill, with its sensational views over the London basin, so that we can reflect on the ages of this landscape from 5000 BC to the present day.

START:	Greenford Underground and Railway Station
FINISH:	Alperton Underground Station
DISTANCE:	4.5 miles (7.5km)
REFRESHMENTS:	Pub, Alperton

From Greenford Station exit, turn left under the railway bridge, then immediately right into Rockware Avenue and continue to the traffic lights. Cross the road obliquely left to the cycle path (signed to Perivale) and turn left along it. In this pleasantly conserved meadowland you can begin to imagine how so much of the area bordering this part of the canal looked when, from the 16th century onwards, it was a major supplier of fodder to London's road and canal horses. Then, Greenford was a rural parish that had grown up around an ancient river crossing, teaming up with other river crossings at Brentford near the Thames and Middle Ford in between the two, near Hanwell.

In the 19th century, Greenford was the local centre of commerce, and by the middle of the century, around 1,000 tons of hay were taken by canal to London each year. Greenford was consumed by suburbia, factories and industrial estates, losing its last shreds of individuality when three major roads were cut through it and the land between was developed in the 1920s and 1930s. The initial trigger for north-west London's development, however, was the 13.5-mile (22.5-km) Paddington Arm of the Grand Junction (later the Grand Union) Canal, which we are just about to join.

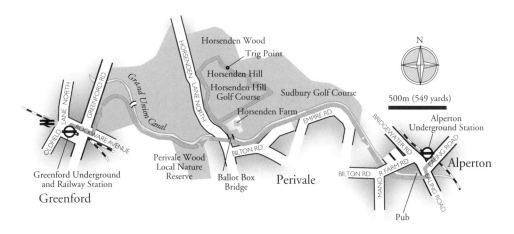

As you follow the cycle path round to the right, the rise of Horsenden Hill provides a backdrop to the meadowland, which, in the summer months, is full of wild flowers, such as mauve and white vetches, and great willowherb. Willows mark the course of a stream and then you will see a wooden footbridge, which announces your approach to the canal. Turn left just before the bridge to turn right beneath it and walk along the towpath.

A Slice of History

The course of the Paddington Arm of the canal is like a core sample of history, piercing the surrounding suburbia and arterial roads. It recalls an age of waterside hay fields, market gardens and a crowded waterway. The 'arm' was completed in the early 19th century, and was busy from the start. It had taken just six years to build, aided by the fact that its course was so level that no locks were needed. The new canal extension provided a cheap, efficient and direct commercial route all the way from Birmingham and the Midlands to the centre of London. Until the Paddington Arm was built, the Grand Junction Canal had terminated much further upstream on the Thames, at Brentford. Barges and narrowboats from Paddington Basin in central London could now continue west and south to join the main Grand Union Canal at Bull's Bridge, then take a right turn to central England. Here, they were joined by boats on their way to or from the Thames at Brentford (see pages 20–27, *Flight of Locks* walk) via the canalized River Brent. The last key commercial link was made when the Regent's Canal was completed in 1820; this extended the Paddington Arm route east to the Thames at Limehouse and the London docklands. When the Grand Junction Canal Company merged with the companies that ran the Regent's and Warwick canals in 1929, the waterway came under the Grand

Union Canal umbrella, and so gained its present name.

The canal here is broad, peaceful and richly bordered with green. The occasional narrowboat chugs peacefully into sight – in contrast to the scene about 150 years ago, when a steady stream of narrowboats transported hay and bricks, which were made in works set up beside the canal to take advantage of the local clay, easy transport and a ready supply of coal transported along the canal. Boats on the return journey to Greenford brought 'mack', which was a mixture of domestic waste and offal, to fertilize the local hay fields and market gardens. Although aggregates, waste and materials for recycling are carried along the canal today, the boats you see are more likely to be for leisure, either purpose-built or with the cargo area converted into living space.

On the Paddington Arm, narrowboats – so named for their slender dimensions (traditionally 7 feet (just over 2m) wide and about 70 feet (20m) long) – would have dominated the scene, in contrast to the broader barges of the Thames waterways. At the beginning of the Canal Age, the boats were cargo carriers operated by teams of men and had no living space at all. Then, with the coming of the railways, boatmen moved on board with their families, combining work and home to cut costs and keep freight prices competitive. Living space was minimal: kitchen, bedroom and living room were crammed into an area just 10 x 7 feet (3 x 2m). Extra cargo space might be provided by a 'butty', an engineless narrowboat that was towed by the lead boat.

Towpath and canal border the fenced-in green area of Perivale Wood Local Nature Reserve on the right, a 27-acre (11-hectare) remnant of the once-mighty, post-glacial Great Middlesex Forest, which was gradually slashed and burned to make way for cultivation and then urban development. Today, it is a Site of Special Scientific Interest (SSSI), but open to the public on just one day a year, at bluebell time in May.

Continue until you reach a small white bridge, about 20 minutes after leaving Greenford Station. This is Ballot Box Bridge, which was built in 1909. Turn right just after the bridge and turn back on yourself to go over it. A farm has been recorded on the site of Horsenden Visitors' Centre on your right since the 16th century. After more than a decade, the farmhouse buildings still do not house the planned information centre and café, although a pleasant garden and picnic tables now occupy the former farmyard. Otherwise there are some faded information boards, a car park and a children's playground. So bypass the gated entrance right, and continue along the lane for a few yards, then turn right into the woods. Almost immediately, take the path to the right of the tarmac path, up some steps to wild grassland. Here, in late summer, are bright splashes of yellow from stands of tall goldenrod, which was once cut and sold as a wound-healing herb. The soft pink-purple blooms of great willowherb, commonly known as codlins-and-cream, add contrast to the colour palette. From June to September, look out for the shrubby dyer's greenweed, with its bright yellow flowers; it is a broomlike member of the pea family from which a yellow pigment was extracted that could be blended with blue woad to make a rich green.

Horsenden Hill

Follow the path that rises slightly, ignoring much steeper side-shoots up- and down-hill, passing through grassland and over a stile with red paint flashes, then into woodland. Meet the tarmac path and immediately turn right up a cobbled path and some earth steps, to reach the summit of Horsenden Hill. It's only 276 feet (85m) above sea level, but through gaps in the trees, you can see the spread of London and suburbia and imagine layers of landscape history. Look down to the arch of the 90,000-seater Wembley Stadium, west as far as Windsor Castle, and from the golf-course slopes, east to the Post Office Tower, London Eye and the City.

The post-glacial forests of oak and shrubby woodland made way for cultivated land and small settlements; then came the vast hay fields and market gardens of the 18th and 19th centuries to feed the ravening London markets. Although their wooden hafts have long since rotted, flint arrowheads from some 7,000 years ago have been found on Horsenden Hill, evidence that the site was on the seasonal hunting and gathering circuit of nomadic Stone Age tribes. Later people took advantage of the hill's defensive position when they began to clear land, cultivate crops for food, rear and keep animals and generally settle down, building a cluster of small round houses. Fragments of their pottery from around 2,500 years ago have been found, and the hill's name – from the Saxon *Horsa's Dun*, meaning 'horse's down' – is thought to refer to these ancient people's reputation as skilled horsemen, though some say that Horsa may have been a Saxon chief.

The forest clearance continued, and more and more of the hill was turned into fields until, by the 14th century, it was producing crops of wheat, barley, corn and rye. Hay fields dominated the hill from the 16th to the 19th century, by which time the local canal transport was playing a key role. Then, in the First World War (1914–18), the hill's prime defensive position came into play when an anti-aircraft gun was positioned on the summit to target German airships. Soon after the war ended, the first wave of factory building began and major roads were constructed in the 1930s. During the Second World War (1939–45), the hill had a searchlight station on the alert for attacks on local factories, which had been turned over to armaments manufacture. Once again the surrounding fields were planted with crops, this time as part of the war effort.

Cross the summit diagonally via the trig point. Wild grassland and woods merge into golf course and your route is, for a while, dictated by the golf course's features. At the seventh tee, take the main path sharp right. Pass the sixth tee and return again to a slice of English countryside in the form of a wood-lined grassy path. At the bottom, turn right to return to the tarmac path, which passes behind the Visitor Centre and its carved entrance, to Ballot Box Bridge. Cross the bridge and return to the towpath to go right towards Alperton. On the right are suburban gardens. Along the towpath you might find a clump of the once-common horseradish plant.

Burgeoning Industry

There's a long stretch now that is attractive enough as you look across to Horsenden Hill, but it can be muddy in winter. It is apt that the last bridge you pass under on this walk is of red brick, for bricks and other building materials, such as sand and gravel, were the most important cargoes along the Paddington Arm in the mid-19th century. There were kilns upstream at West Drayton, Yiewsley and Hayes, and the opening of the canal transformed the farming village of Alperton, which in 1805 consisted of just 21 houses and 14 farms. Soon, shipments of coal (canal transport cut the price of coal by half), hay and construction materials were being handled here and brick- and tile-making industries were established nearby. A pleasure-boat service ferried Londoners on a day trip to the Pleasure Boat pub, which overlooks the opposite bank of the canal, and this became a favourite resort of anglers. All too soon, however, Alperton became the most industrialized village in Wembley, and the odours of pigswill and dung from the remaining farms mingled with industrial smoke and a local sewage farm.

As you pass under the red-brick bridge, towards a blue high-rise block ahead, look down to the canal bank for the rusting remains of a stop gate mechanism, which is now partly hidden by vegetation. The stop gate, with its downstream partner, was a guard against the canal water bursting its banks in the event of a bomb strike. If this were to happen, the gates could be lowered to stop the flow of water and reduce flooding downstream. Just before the next (concrete) bridge, peel off to the right and up the steps; head left across the bridge and take the first right, Ealing Road, to Alperton Underground Station.

Opposite: *Ballot Box Bridge crosses the Grand Union Canal and leads to the view-point of Horsenden Hill. The bridge is so called because in the 19th century there was a ballot box located nearby where boatmen could cast their votes in an election.*

A FLIGHT OF LOCKS: GRAND UNION CANAL, BRENTFORD–HANWELL

Summary: The suburb of Brentford is the gateway to the Thames from the inland waterways of England, once an important meeting point of road, rail, canal and river. It was a fortified ford during the Roman occupation (AD 43–84) and after the 18th century it was once a market garden for London. If you're used to seeing the area from the A4 road, this is a walk that takes you through surprising hidden gems in suburbia, past muddy banks and herons, covered wharves and – if you go in late summer or early autumn – lots of blackberries to where you can see a flight of locks in action at Hanwell.

START:	Kew Bridge Railway Station
FINISH:	Hanwell Railway Station
DISTANCE:	6 miles (10km)
REFRESHMENTS:	Waterman's Arts Centre; The Fox pub at Hanwell Locks

Turn right out of Kew Bridge Station and go along Kew Bridge Road for a couple of hundred yards to the tall brick tower on the right. This is the Kew Bridge Steam Museum, formerly the Grand Junction Water Works Company. From 1838 until 1944, water was pumped from the Thames by massive steam engines housed in this building, then cleaned and treated before being pumped onwards to households and factories from Sunbury to Kensington.

Nature Trail
From the museum, turn left back towards Kew Bridge, cross the road at the traffic lights and go down the slip road on the right-hand side of the bridge. Continue down to a paved square on the bank of the River Thames and turn right to follow a leafy path lined with buddleia, balsam, willow and the miniature garden plots of moored houseboats. At a cobbled circle with a semicircular iron bench, go up the asphalt path in front of the apartment blocks, then turn right to go up the steps to the main road. Turn left, and after only a few yards, past Victoria Steps car park, turn left again to enter Waterside Park. The path is high

above a muddy backwater of the Thames that seeps behind the islands of Brentford Ait and Lots Ait and is littered with neglected vessels, some supporting spontaneous wildflife gardens. The islands have trees thick and lush in high summer. Beyond the church tower to the right, the path meets the red-brick building of the Waterman's Arts Centre; cut up right to the terrace for a drink or continue along the path to the end of the building, turn right down some steps at the back, and right into the car park. Turn left out of the car park, right up the stepped path to the main road and cross it into Ealing Road. Take the first left into Albany Road, then second right (Brook Road South) and first left into Grosvenor Road. At the end, go straight across the recreation ground along an avenue of lime trees and past a Victorian fountain into St Paul's Road. Go straight ahead, past the little Victorian school on the left with its separate entrances for boys and girls, to the wide road called Half Acre; turn right and cross over, then turn left into an elegant tree-lined residential avenue called The Butts: 'The Butts Estate' is engraved into a stone plaque on the wall at the entrance.

Victorian residential architecture precedes a delightful enclave of Georgian and Queen Anne houses, some dating back to the 1680s. They recall a time when Brentford was a grand place to live, close enough to London but a town of some standing in its own right. In Victorian times, traffic into London increased, as more and more produce was taken from the surrounding farms and market gardens along the long-established main route over the River Brent. Brentford became notorious for the mud churned up on its overused roads, and for its concentration of breweries and other factories.

The Grand Junction

Cross the square (a former marketplace) diagonally to the far left corner before turning left into a road called Market Place. Continue straight ahead, passing Brentford Magistrates Court on the right, and turn right at the main road. In a couple of minutes you cross the bridge over the River Brent and turn right on the far side of the bridge to Brentford Lock, the first indication that the river is not in its natural state. The Brent was not navigable until 1794, when it was tamed and straightened into an extension of the Grand Junction Canal, the final link in a through-route between the Midlands and the River Thames. The Grand Junction's engineer was William Jessop. His brief was to create a waterway that would slice 60 miles (100km) off the trade route between London and Birmingham. He went further than this, providing a solution to the usual bottlenecks at locks by making his locks double width at 14 feet (over 4m), so that two 7-foot (2-m) wide narrowboats could squeeze through simultaneously. It also made the locks accessible to the wider 70-ton barges that worked the downstream waterways and the Thames.

At Brentford Lock, barges and their freight were checked in and their operators charged a toll based on type of boat and weight of cargo. Later, in 1859, the Great Western Railway, carrying freight from Bristol and from western and southern England, was extended to Brentford, and the surrounding area – especially between the lock and the Thames (see pages 170–77, *Thames-Side Retreats* walk) – became densely packed with warehouses, workshops, freight sheds and a railway marshalling yard. All gradually fell into disuse in the mid-20th century, but since the 1970s the area has been redeveloped to provide desirable waterside housing.

Shadowing the M4

Soon the path goes interestingly under cover beneath overhanging warehouses. This was the Brentford Depot, a freight terminal at which barges and cargo carriers (called lighters) from the downstream Thames and the docks, which were too wide for the canals of central England, transferred their loads on to narrowboats. Even into the early 20th century, 20,000 narrowboats loaded up here each year. Suddenly, the canal–river is green with healthy brambles and unrestrained vegetation, until it becomes a stretch bordered by office blocks, from which office-workers spill at sunny lunchtimes to eat their sandwiches on the grassy canal banks.

At the next lock, Clitheroe's (named after a former Sheriff of Middlesex and owner of nearby Boston Manor Park), look to the far side of the canal–river, where there's a glimpse of the old river in its near-natural state bypassing the canal. This usefully channels overflow water from above the upper lock gate. For a time, the canal is hemmed in by railway tracks, the A4 road and the M4 motorway.

Cross the river at the iron Gallows Bridge, which may have been built by Thomas Telford (1757–1834), another of those great 19th-century engineers. The bridge, which bears the Grand Union Canal Company insignia, has a rough surface to enable canal horses to grip it and takes its name from a nearby gallows where highwaymen were hanged. Willow trees and meadow flowers soothe the eye, but the roar of the motorway is never far away and the din of an overhead train may intrude as you pass under a mainline railway bridge. Once you've finally passed beneath the motorway, which has been your companion for too long, peace falls and you arrive at Osterley Lock, where there is a nature reserve and picnic site. Cross an iron walkway over the weir backwater and head under a platform road bridge to curve north-west. Playing fields inland were created over an infill site from river-straightening excavations. Continue past a milepost – '91 miles to Braunston', a Northamptonshire canal stop – and a severe corrugated iron warehouse on the

Opposite: *The skeletal frames are those of former warehouses that stretched over the water in the heyday of the former Brentford freight depot, where wide barges from the Thames transferred loads to narrowboats for the journey inland along the canals.*

ALWYNE RD

CAMPBELL ROAD
Hanwell Railway Station

Hanwell

St Bernard's Hospital

N

Windmill
Bridge

500m (549 yards)

Hanwell Locks

Fox PH

TRUMPERS WAY

Playing fields

River Brent

Osterley Lock

Picnic site

M4

Grand

Union Canal

Gallows Bridge

Clitheroe's Lock

TRANSPORT AVENU

opposite bank. Soon you come to a
row of houses on the right and a
turning to the right leads to the Fox pub.

The Marvel of Hanwell Flight

In the old pre-canalization days, the river
flowed shallow here, and cattle crossed over to
Green Lane towards Hanwell village. Soon the
unnavigable river joins the canal, and you reach
the pièce de résistance of the walk: the Hanwell
Locks – a 'flight' of locks, which was completed in 1796
and is now a designated ancient monument. A flight is the
collective term for a number of locks that take a canal over a steep
gradient. A set of locks even steeper than the 53 feet (16m) over $^1/_3$
mile (0.5km) flight at Hanwell is known as a staircase. The locks are
indeed like a series of stepped chambers, filled or emptied in succession to
raise or lower the boats to the next level. It's easy on foot, but can take a canal
boat over $1^1/_2$ hours to negotiate the full flight of six locks. Each lock chamber has

gates at either end; the water level in the chambers is adjusted by opening and shutting paddles over the holes in the gate and in the ground paddle, which spans the width of the lock at the bottom. When a chamber is empty, you can see the culverts through which water from the upper level will gush to fill the next level down.

Keep an eye open for the numbers of the locks, and cross over Lock 97 to the restored side pond. Side ponds are cisterns that store water for topping up the locks – for a single chamber might consume 50,000 gallons (227,000 litres) of water as it fills. Some of the side ponds are covered with a billiard-table film of weed in summer, which has the effect of deoxygenating the water, and there are health-hazard signs to dissuade you from taking a dip. Nevertheless, it is hard to imagine now, but at the end of the 19th century, pollution was so bad along this stretch of the canal that barges were ploughing through lumps of raw, black, gaseous sewage and stirring up foul-smelling silt from the canal bed. Barge men complained that they could not bear to eat on board when cruising through the Hanwell area.

The high wall bordering the right of the towpath after Lock 94 enclosed the former County Lunatic Asylum, which opened in the 1830s. In its day the asylum was innovative in its treatment of psychiatric patients: nursing staff were appropriately trained and paid, and patients were treated with affectionate care and attention. In the hospital's 44 acres (18 hectares) of land there was a brewery, a bakery and a farm where patients cultivated the land, making the hospital self-sufficient in fruit, vegetables and meat. The hospital also had its own canal-side dock, where surplus produce was shipped to London markets and coal was unloaded for the hospital boilers. The ghost of the former dock entrance can be seen in the form of a low-level concrete-covered arch in the brick wall; the rectangular holes just before it were for fire hoses. On the opposite bank, at Lock 93, is a canal pound and at Lock 96 there is an early 19th-century lock cottage, from which the keeper checked that the locks and traffic were operating smoothly.

On From the Flight

After the sixth lock, the canal narrows to pass under Windmill Lane. This is the site of the last major project undertaken by the Victorian engineer Isambard Kingdom Brunel (1806–59), and is a combination of road, canal and rail routes. Each of the three routes enters the intersection point at a

Weeping willow

different angle and at a different level: Brunel's metal-beamed trough, which you can see above the towpath, carries the road, while he designed huge brick arches to support the Great Western Railway through a cutting underneath both road and canal.

Retrace your steps back down the flight of locks and take the path left at Lock 96, where canal and original river separate. Your walk continues along a leafy stretch of the real River Brent. Pass under the bridge or cross the Uxbridge Road. Opposite are allotments; in the past the meadows were common land with thriving watercress cultivation. Continue along the west bank of the river towards Brunel's magnificent Wharncliffe Viaduct (see pages 125–29, *Ribbon of Green* walk). Cross the footbridge just before the viaduct and turn right. Turn right again and left into a little park. Turn left under the viaduct arch, right along Golden Manor, right again and follow Campbell Road right to Hanwell Railway Station.

SHORT CUTS TO LIMEHOUSE: LIMEHOUSE CUT AND HERTFORD UNION CANAL

Summary: Limehouse Basin is where the inland canals meet the River Thames and the world beyond. We take a circular route from the basin to follow a couple of former short cuts for trade and cargo: the Limehouse Cut, between the River Lea and the Thames, which bypasses the loop round the Isle of Dogs, and the Hertford Union Canal. The area has seen better – and worse – times, but it is steeped in industrial history. Much of the path is gravel and/or concrete and, although the route might be a bit grim on a grey day, this is an all-weather walk.

START AND FINISH:	Limehouse DLR Station
DISTANCE:	6 miles (10km)
REFRESHMENTS:	The Narrow pub, Limehouse; Palm Tree pub, Mile End

From the bottom of the steps down from Limehouse DLR Station, head south along Branch Road, keeping left where it forks, and at the junction with Horseferry Road, turn right, passing a large-scale pink and cream brick building with red paintwork. This is the approach to the four-lane Limehouse Tunnel, which runs under the Limehouse Basin and was completed in 1994. Follow Horseferry Road round to the left and turn left along Narrow Street. At the end of Sun Wharf warehouses on the right, turn right down an alley to a broad sweep of the Thames. Turn left and follow the Thames Path to The Narrow pub and dining-room overlooking the entrance of Limehouse Basin. This Georgian-style building is in fact Edwardian (c.1905–10), and was once the dock's Custom House.

The riverfront here was already bustling by Tudor times. It was the age of exploration, and Sir Walter Raleigh (1552–1618) sailed from Limehouse in 1595 on a quest to the New World and the gold it was rumoured to harbour.

The name Limehouse hails from the 14th century, when lime kilns were

Bottom Lock

White Post Lane

Middle Lock

Lee Navigation

Top Lock

Victoria Park

Three Colt Bridge

GUNMAKER'S LANE

A12

Old Ford Lock

River Lea

Olympic Park

Hertford Union Canal

PARNELL ROAD

River Lea

Greenway

OLD FORD ROAD

GROVE ROAD

GROVE ROAD

Palm Tree PH

ROMAN ROAD

Mile End Park

Regent's Canal

HIGH ST

BOW RD

THREE MILL LANE

BLACKWALL TUNNEL NORTHERN APPROACH A12

Bromley-By-Bow Underground Station

Mile End Lock

MILE END ROAD

Mile End Park

Bow Locks

COPPERFIELD RD

VIOLET RD

MORRIS RD

Ragged School Museum

Jonson's Lock

BEN JONSON ROAD

Salmon Lane Lock

Commercial Road Lock

Limehouse Railway Station

BRANCH ROAD

BEKESBOURNE STREET

SALMON LANE

Limehouse Cut

BURDETT ROAD

COMMERCIAL ROAD A13

N

DLR

Limehouse DLR Station

St Anne's Church

TUNNEL APPROACH

Limehouse Basin

LIMEHOUSE TUNNEL

HORSEFERRY ROAD

NARROW STREET

River Thames

Sun Wharf

500m (549 yards)

worked nearby. Stone was burned and reduced to quicklime powder, which was used in building mortar and, later, for making pottery and as a disinfectant. The constant traffic of sailors from around the world created a cosmopolitan community, including London's first Chinatown, which grew up nearby in the mid-19th century and became notorious for its opium dens. In Victorian times the area was overcrowded, insanitary and dangerous.

Regent's Canal Dock

Go round The Narrow pub and up some steps to the road; turn right to cross the entrance to Limehouse Basin and turn immediately left, signposted Limehouse Cut, Lea Valley Walk and Three Mills.

Regent's Canal Dock – as Limehouse Basin was known before 1969 – was excavated from marshy, low-lying land in the 1820s. Instead of today's prospect of desirable waterside residences, the dock was crammed with coasters, short-haul sea-trading ships and lighters that had 'lightened' the loads of ocean-going vessels moored downriver; quays were lined with wharves and warehouses and peopled with gangs of coal-whippers, porters, stevedores and bargees. You could walk directly across the dock using the barges, so tightly were they packed. Coal, iron, grain and timber were among the raw materials and supplies that came via the Thames and London's bigger docks to be transferred to canal barges and narrowboats at Limehouse. The canal boats left the dock in the north-east corner to join the Regent's Canal and on to deliver their goods to north and west London and the Midlands.

From the late 18th century, and before railways took over in the second half of the 19th century, canals provided the cheapest, most efficient method of transporting bulky goods. At their peak in the late 18th century, there was a 4,250-mile (6,840-km) network of navigable rivers and canals, linking centres of production and industry throughout Britain. Despite competing road and rail transport, the Regent's Canal and the dock were still in use in the 20th century, but the dock's commercial life had fizzled out more or less completely by 1969 and its name changed to Limehouse Basin. The area was neglected and rundown until the early 1980s, when the British Waterways joined forces with London Docklands Development Corporation in a regeneration programme.

As you round the first corner of the basin, look straight ahead across the water. In the gaps between tall blocks of flats, the tower of a Catholic church is topped by a statue instead of the usual cross; it is known as the 'steering Christ', because it served as a navigational aid for sailors coming into the Basin. To the left, a brick accumulator tower marks the coming of hydraulic power, developed by William Armstrong (1810–1900) in 1846. Heavy steam-powered iron cylinders inside the tower maintained the water pressure that provided power to operate the dock's lock gates, a swing bridge and cranes. Locks maintained a constant water level in the dock, as the level of the Thames fluctuated with the tides.

Continue along the brick path round the basin, keeping to the lower path and passing under the iron bridge. At the junction turn left under another footbridge, following signs for Limehouse Cut and River Lea Valley. Ahead is St Anne's Church, completed in 1724 to a design by Nicholas Hawksmoor (1661–1736), one-time clerk to Sir Christopher Wren (1591–1650) and later architect of many distinctive City churches. The church's size and striking tower not only reflected Limehouse's wealth and status at the time, but also served as a landmark for mariners en route to the Pool of London.

Along the Cut

Walk along Limehouse Cut for a rather featureless and relentlessly straight 1¹/₂ miles (2.5km) – but just before going beneath the first road bridge, look up left to the fortress-like 'Mission', built as lodgings for sailors in the 1920s, now luxury apartments. Be grateful that the foul-smelling effluents are no longer present. Overcrowding in the city centre and mid-19th-century pollution laws forced factories to relocate, and this is one of the places they came to, making good use of the canal to transport their goods, bring in coal supplies and dump their waste. Limehouse Cut fared worse than other areas, with gas works and chemical-processing factories, lime works and pet-food manufacturers. The bridge beneath the chemical works was known as Stinkinghouse, a description that could probably have applied to the whole stretch. A local recalls his great uncle loading his barge with fish guts discarded from Billingsgate Fish Market and rowing along the cut to deliver his strong-smelling cargo to the pet-food factory. Anyone who fell in the cut was likely to contract a nasty, if not fatal, water-borne disease.

The original purpose of the canal was to provide a short cut between the River Lea to the east and the Thames at Limehouse. This convenient route, which bypasses the Isle of Dogs' meander in the Thames, was actually planned in the late 16th century during Elizabeth I's reign, though the cut was finally dug only in 1776. Even then it was still something of a novelty: the pioneering Bridgwater Canal from Wigan to Manchester had been completed just a few years before. Originally, the cut led straight to the Thames at Limehouse, but in 1968 it was diverted to Limehouse Basin. Today, the Victorian factories have gone, and what we now see is the odd surviving, grubby warehouse, office buildings, housing and the occasional decorative steel pier built in the form of a ship's bows – certainly some improvement on the cut's noxious past. Look out for rafts of aquatic plants and an interesting variety of floating nesting boxes to attract waterfowl; some boxes have ramps or slides, others have gabled roofs. You will certainly see moorhens, and you may spot a cormorant.

The Lea Meets the Lee

After about 20 minutes of walking along Limehouse Cut, a boardwalk path under the A12 leads to the meeting with the Lee Navigation. Cross a stepped bridge over Bow Locks and walk through a welcome green ribbon of an island between the Lee Navigation and Bow Creek. After passing beneath a railway bridge, the incongruously picturesque Three Mills is on the right (see pages 130–37, *Old Rivers for New* walk), where the pull of the tide was utilised to power a flour mill and distillery. Go up and left to cross the bridge over Three Mill Lane, and turn right back down to the waterside path along the west bank of the Lee Navigation.

The River Lea, in its natural state, wound a leisurely 70-mile (117-km) path from its source near Luton to the River Thames at Bow Creek, downriver of the Isle of Dogs. The waterway was deep enough for Danish invaders to sail up as far north as Hertford in AD 896, but there they became stuck, for King Alfred the Great had split the main stream of the Lea into three channels, which were too shallow for navigation. There is a long history of waterborne trade on the river, too: malt and corn were transported from Hertford in flat-bottomed barges, which had to negotiate the river's uneven, long-winded and inefficient course. In the 16th century, the first section of the Lee Navigation was cut, and locks were built resulting in a direct, reliable and navigable waterway.

Many local farmers and carriers who carted their goods by road felt so threatened by the cheaper water transport provided by the Lee Navigation that they sabotaged river banks, locks and towpath bridges. But the die was cast, and the system of straight channels and locks was extended to include Limehouse Cut in the 18th century. A rash of factories set up along the new waterways, which could now receive raw materials from London and dispatch their finished goods with ease. By the 20th century, barges were taking coal to Hackney Power Station, timber to furniture factories beyond Tottenham, copper to small-arms factories upriver at Enfield (home of the Lee Enfield rifle) and oranges to marmalade factories at Ware. It wasn't until the 1950s that such traffic ceased.

Bazalguette and Duckett

A new gravel path continues under the A11/Bow flyover and then crosses the Navigation to follow the east bank. We are now bordering the London 2012

Opposite: *A 1906 chimney built to ventilate an underground sewer is just one interesting landmark at this point on the Regents Canal. To the left is Mile End Park, created from the ashes of World War II bombing, and in the distance, the glittering commercial centre of Canary Wharf, which arose from redundant docklands.*

Cormorant

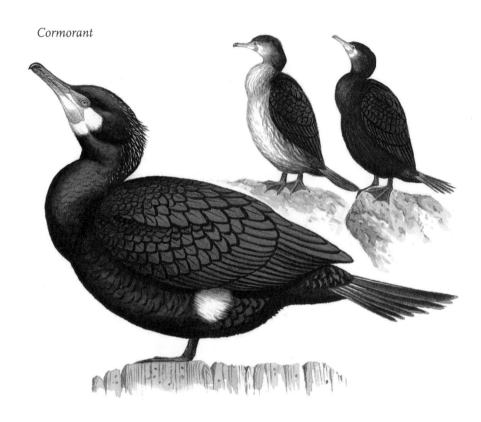

Olympic Park, which continues a process of Olympic 'Legacy' transformation into a mix of sport and leisure, commercial and residential development. Just beyond a sign for 'Greenway', go under a bridge of metal girders carrying a giant pipe, which is a sewer of 1860s vintage. Greenway is the genteel modern name for the path that follows the route of the Northern Outfall Sewer. This sewer intercepted raw waste from a million households and industries which had once gone straight into the Thames, often bubbling up through the floorboards of poorer homes en route. Salmon and swans disappeared from the Thames, and bodies salvaged from the wrecked *Princess Alice* (a pleasure cruiser that collided with a steam collier ship in 1865 resulting in a death toll of around 600 people) were covered in vile slime. Outbreaks of cholera were common. In 1858, the year of 'The Great Stink', curtains in the Houses of Parliament were soaked in disinfectant every day to combat the stench rising from the river. It was a man born in Enfield, in the Lea Valley, who solved the problem. Joseph Bazalguette (1819–91) Chief Engineer to London's Metropolitan Board of Works and the brains behind the Victoria and Albert Embankments (see pages 151–60, *Bridging the Thames* walk), oversaw the construction of 1,300 miles (2,170km) of sewer pipe with back-up settling tanks and pumping stations.

On the opposite bank, an old warehouse is still standing. Just beyond it, turn left to go over the footbridge across the Old River Lea (looking upstream to a perspective now dominated by the decapitated Olympic Stadium). Bear right to go straight along the right bank of the Lee Navigation, passing Old Ford Lock on the left. As its name suggests, Old Ford was once – from the Roman occupation – a shallow river crossing on the route between London and Essex. Follow the Lee to the next bridge, where you go up onto White Post Lane. Turn left across it and left again back to the opposite bank. The waterway makes a right-angle turn, and becomes the Hertford Union Canal, all 1¼ miles (2.1km) of it. There's a bigger view of the former Olympic Park, garish graffiti, and apple blossoms in spring at an adjacent garden centre. The canal is known as Duckett's Cut, after the man who funded it, Sir George Duckett. It was opened in 1830, enabling the tidal River Lea to be bypassed altogether and creating a direct link between the Regent's and Grand Union canals and the Lee Navigation. However, the canal diverted precious water from the Regent's Canal and was closed during the 1850s, although it was later added to the Regent's Canal network.

London's First Park

Because of the low level of traffic on the Hertford Union (see pages 38–43, *Barges Go West* walk), its locks are single: only one boat could go through at a time, unlike the two-way system of twin locks that was a feature of the Regent's Canal, which you will soon meet. You pass Bottom and Middle locks, and then, just before the Parnell Road Bridge (also known as Homerton Footpath Bridge), is the attractive – and rare – Top, or Upper, Lock. It has two sets of double wooden gates, the lower of which has unusual and quite fragile cast-iron balance beams; the beams are infilled with concrete and have reinforcing iron bands. The lock cottages were built at the same time as the canal.

Beyond the Parnell Road Bridge, the houses on the far bank may not be particularly special to look at, but they enjoy a prospect of both the canal and of London's oldest public park. Victoria Park was laid out in 1840, at the beginning of the eponymous queen's reign. Look down to the water for relief from more residential development to nesting rafts for moorhens and ducks, then pass by older properties with canal-side gardens and a Victorian school with an ornate weathervane. The next bridge you pass under is Three Colt Bridge, also known as Gunmaker's Lane Bridge. As with Parnell Bridge, it owes the extra effort taken over its design to being part of the Victoria Park development and is listed for conservation.

Continue beneath Old Ford Road and Grove Road; opposite are 19th-century warehouses. At the junction with the Regent's Canal, turn left. The cobbled track over the bridge gave barge horses a grip on the slopes – maybe sparks flew from a combination of effort and iron shoe, for the cobbles were known as 'scorchers'. As you walk along this part of the Regent's Canal, look for the occasional cutaway canal edge, where there are cobbled ramps beneath the water which a horse could scramble up if it fell in. Perhaps to limit the possibility of such an accident happening and to avoid traffic jams, it was illegal to let horses drink from the canals; instead, water troughs were provided at points away from the towpath.

Changing Landscapes

Now, as you pass through Mile End, you will see canal-side landscapes of varying success, from urban parks with overcrowded flowerbeds to wilder nature reserves complete with ponds, and a possible pub stop at the Palm Tree pub. Once there were factories here producing chocolates, shirts, chemicals and lime juice, and vast corrugated-iron warehouses overhanging the canal for loading ships under shelter.

At Mile End Lock, a cubist glass extension has been added to restored Georgian cottages on the opposite bank, just before Mile End Road crosses the canal. You can take a parallel route through the bordering Mile End Park, for on the opposite bank there is little to see for a time but old warehouses and offices. Soon, you will see the landmark of Canary Wharf Tower in the distance, a vibrant contrast to the abandoned air of much of this stretch.

Just off to the left, in Copperfield Road, is the Ragged School Museum. In 1895, this building was the largest of Dr Barnardo's 148 Ragged Schools in London and gave free lessons to poor children and free meals in winter. The red-brick chimney on your left soon after this point was built in 1906 as a ventilation shaft to air the low-level sewer which extended from the western suburb of Hammersmith and linked up with Joseph Bazalguette's great Northern Outfall Sewer.

A run of locks starts with Jonson's Lock just before Ben Jonson Road, then Salmon Lane Lock, with its lock cottages and tubular footbridge – giant pipes running beneath Commercial Road Bridge – and the Commercial Road Lock. You will see a viaduct, which was designed by George Stephenson (1781–1848), the man who introduced the public to steam trains with the *Rocket* in 1829. The viaduct opened in 1840 and was one of the first railways to connect to the London docks; it now carries part of the Docklands Light Railway system. The section over the canal was roofed to eliminate the possibility of the steam trains passing overhead showering sparks on to barges and setting fire to their cargo.

The canal reaches its destination in Limehouse Basin. Turn right and follow the basin's north side, which runs parallel to the viaduct carrying the DLR line. Look to your left to see the moored narrowboats, which are colourful, clean and for leisure use only. At the road, turn right to Limehouse DLR Station.

BARGES GO WEST: REGENT'S CANAL, MILE END–CALEDONIAN ROAD

Summary: We follow an imaginary, horse-drawn barge on the first leg of its journey along the Regent's Canal to the Paddington Basin. The canal provided a link between the River Thames and London's docklands, taking imported goods such as timber, rice and exotic fruit into the heart of England, and carrying coal from the Midlands to coal merchants and gas works along its banks. Our destination is the Canal Museum, where you can see model boats, archive films about working life on the waterways and many artefacts.

START:	Mile End Underground Station
FINISH:	King's Cross Underground and Railway Station
DISTANCE:	4$^1/_3$ miles (7.2km)
REFRESHMENTS:	Mile End, pubs at road level above canal; small café at the Canal Museum

The Regent's Canal was constructed between 1812 and 1820 to connect the Thames at Limehouse to Paddington Basin, the terminus of the Grand Union Canal (see pages 14–19, *Hay and Bricks* walk). Our imaginary barge has loaded up at Limehouse Basin, and is on its way along the 8½-mile (14.2-km) Regent's Canal to join the Grand Union Canal at Paddington Basin. Our journey, though, begins at Mile End Lock. Coming downstream, broad, flat, unadorned and begrimed with fine black dust, we pass barges with oblong holds that take up most of their length and which are filled end-to-end with conical piles of coal.

A Barge Reverie
From Mile End Station, turn left and join the canal at the access point on the north side of Mile End Road. Turn right along the towpath to Mile End Lock,

Opposite: The approach to the ½-mile (835m) Islington Tunnel, where the barge horses were led overland while two men 'walked' the barge through the tunnel by pushing their legs against the side walls.

where, on the opposite bank, the Georgian lock-keeper's cottage abuts in startling contrast to an overhang of modern architecture. Pass under a railway bridge to go alongside the Mile End equivalent of Little Venice, with a stream of houseboat moorings.

Look out for canal boats of differing widths. In the canals of central England, 7-foot (2-m) wide narrowboats dominated the older, narrower canals, but here, on the Regent's Canal, barges were more common. They were short-haul carriers and no valuable cargo space was taken up with living cabins or engines; as the barges were also double the width of narrowboats, they had four times the weight capacity – up to 100 tons. One bargeman steered, while a second looked after a horse, which hauled a barge along the straight, smooth waters of a canal and could move around 50 times the weight of a horse-drawn wagon on an unmetalled road. Canal horses needed around 8lb (3.5kg) of oats a day to maintain energy levels, so a nosebag or bowl was slung around the animal's neck so that it could feed while plodding along. Canal horses also had to be shod every two weeks – twice as often as other working horses. Medium-sized cobs were the usual choice of animal, as they were densely built and strong but small enough to go under the canal bridges.

Some barges towed 'butties' to double their cargo space, although from the mid-19th century these were sometimes hauled along in a long train by a steam tug and from the 1950s by a small tractor on the towpath. Nevertheless, horses were still seen working on the Regent's Canal as late as the 1950s.

Continue under a railway bridge, heading north along the towpath with the long, narrow 79-acre (32 hectares) Mile End Park on the right. The Park rose from the ashes of a Second World War bombsite. The Palm Tree pub, set back from the towpath before the next road bridge, is a lone survivor from a residential area that was devastated by the first V1 flying bomb ('Doodlebug') in

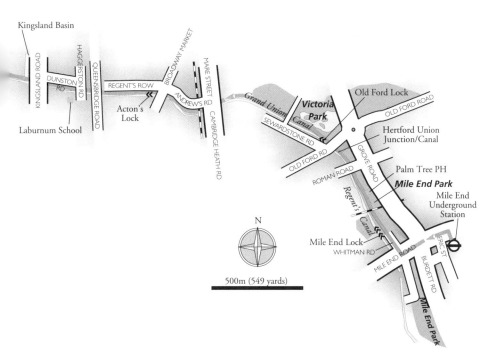

1944 and earlier air attacks. The naturalized landscaping and lakes of the Ecology Park have attracted rare orchids and insects, including flourishing populations of waterbirds, dragonflies and damselflies. Keep straight ahead at a bridge where the Hertford Union Canal comes in from the right (see pages 28–37, *Short Cuts to Limehouse*).

Immediately after the bridge is Old Ford Lock (not to be confused with Old Ford Lock on the Lee Navigation). If our barge encountered another boat coming in the opposite direction, both vessels could use the lock simultaneously, as the Regent's Canal locks were built in pairs to cater for two-way traffic, which cut waiting time. The secondary locks were closed after the Second World War, following an unfortunate incident when somebody left a whole run of paddle gates open, causing floods at King's Cross Station. Today, Camden Lock (see pages 44–50, *Regency Waterway* walk) is the only fully operative 'twin'.

From Old Ford Lock is a lovely stretch, bordered by Victoria Park, where swards of green lined with mature trees run parallel to the towpath. As you pass under the bridges en route, look out for the metal reinforcements on the corners – these protected the brickwork from being worn by tow ropes. Look down into the water, too, for there are many submarine ramps in cutaway sections of the canal bank, designed for horses to climb up should they fall in. At Mare Street, where brick arches conceal heavy metal girders, there is an iron ring that once supported a rubbing pole for the towing ropes to turn round.

Gasometers rise ahead. Gasworks and canals went together, because of the ready supply of prodigious quantities of coal needed to produce the gas. You begin to get an idea of how and why 19th-century London had blackened buildings and a serious pollution problem.

By the bridges, look out for more remnants of transport history: the lock-keeper's cottage at Acton's Lock, and just beyond, before Queensbridge, the rare remains of a cobbled street. The Kingsland Basin, at the next bridge, was one of London's largest 'basins', made in the 1820s to extend canal-side warehousing facilities. Tropical grasses have been found growing in this area: exotic plants are quite often found beside canals, self-grown from seeds attached to passing cargoes from foreign fields. Cross a cobbled bridge over the entrance to Kingsland Basin.

More horse ramps appear on the canal bank, and just before the Whitmore Road bridge there is an attractive row of two- and three-storey warehouses. After the bridge, new residential development has brought with it extensive canal-side landscape improvements and a new footbridge. Look up left just before a girder railway bridge, to Rosemary Works, once a stationery producer, now a primary school. Just beyond the bridge is an arc of giant sewer pipe, sometimes painted in rainbow colours. Carry on, past Sturt's Lock and a classic Victorian factory chimney on the left. Walk past the canal-like cut of Wenlock Basin, and waterside mosaics. Wenlock Basin heralds the approach of the main concentration of warehouses on the Regent Canal.

Just after Wharf Road, City Road Basin opens out on the left. This basin was the canal's main centre for the transferral of goods, such as timber, paper, flour, marble and rubber to the specialist warehouses and factories that lined the quays. Our imaginary barge might have stopped here overnight, as there were stables for the horses. The base of a modern office block curves right down into the water, blocking part of the paired lock.

A Spot of Legging

The towpath comes to an end just before the Islington Tunnel. We, like the canal horse, must go overland, while barges were 'legged' through the tunnel. It was handy if there was someone who could lead the horse, for two men were needed to push their legs against the side walls of the tunnel and 'walk' the barge along. They lay, backs down, on boards that were hooked across the sides of the barge. The journey of more than half a mile (835m) took over an hour and, if motorized narrowboats were also using the tunnel, the leggers were in danger of being overcome by fumes. Nevertheless, even when a steam tug was introduced in 1826 to tow the barges through, many still preferred to 'leg' it rather than pay for the tug.

Go up the signed, sloping footpath from the towpath, then right along Colebrooke Row with its tall Georgian terraces. Cross the road and turn left at Charlton Place and go straight up to meet Islington High Street. Cross to the Business Design Centre and keep to the left of it, following the bend left then turning right into Bromfield Street. Turn left, then go right to pass a supermarket left and a park right, continuing to main Barnsbury Road. Cross the road, turn right and then left into Maygood Street. At the end of the street, take the narrow footpath and follow the school playground round to the right. The path emerges by the Duchess of Kent pub; go straight down and turn left into Muriel Street. Look out on the right for the iron gates as these mark the return to the canal towpath.

Continue to the Caledonian Road bridge, go under it and turn right to go up to the road, then right again to cross the canal. Take the first right, then third left to see the Canal Museum on the right. The museum itself is in a warehouse that used to store ice. In pre-refrigeration days, ice was big business on the Regent's Canal. Large blocks of ice were cut from Norwegian fjords, carried in the holds of sailing ships to the Thames and transferred to barges in the Regent's Canal Dock (Limehouse Basin); from there, the ice was transported to the warehouse in Battlebridge Basin, which the museum overlooks. Here, overseen by former ice-cream maker Carlo Gatti, it was unloaded into deep wells with sandy floors through which the meltwater filtered.

To reach King's Cross Underground and Railway Station, turn right out of the museum, right along Wharfdale Road and left along York Way. The next walk takes you along the next stretch of the Regent's Canal.

REGENCY WATERWAY: REGENT'S CANAL, CALEDONIAN ROAD– LITTLE VENICE

Summary: In this section of the Regent's Canal route, industry was confined to activity on the waterway itself, for its banks are bordered by some of the most elegant Regency houses in London, rather than warehouses and factories. We pass through trendy Camden, skim past London Zoo and Regent's Park and wander through Little Venice, gaining insight into how canals were built and into an ambitious bit of Regency town planning.

START:	King's Cross Railway and Underground Station
FINISH:	Paddington Railway and Underground Station
DISTANCE:	4¼ miles (7.1km)
REFRESHMENTS:	Canal Museum café; Camden Lock Market; Paddington Station

From the Euston Road exit of King's Cross Rail Station, turn left into York Way, then take the third right into Wharfdale Road. Take the second left into New Wharf Road to pass the Canal Museum (see page 43). Turn right, then left across the canal at Caledonian Road. Turn left just after the bridge to join the towpath. You will see immediately Battlebridge Basin, which the Canal Museum overlooks, on the opposite bank. The basin was open for business from 1822, and past industries included beer bottling, a timber yard and warehouses for corn, salt and imported fruit used for making jam and preserves. Its name is a corruption of Broad Ford Bridge, an ancient crossing on the long-lost Fleet River.

Canal and Railway in Tandem
The restored cast-iron Maiden Lane Bridge carries York Way, the busy road that leads north from King's Cross Station. The canal enjoyed a brief renaissance

during the Second World War, taking pressure off the overworked railways, and stop gates were installed at this point to prevent water from flooding into the tunnels in the event of the canal being bombed. The gates would have been lowered to halt the flow of upstream water into the bomb-damaged area, thus reducing the danger of flooding in the two railway tunnels that had been cut far beneath the waterway in 1852 to carry trains to King's Cross. There was a canal extension to the King's Cross goods shed, although it has long been bricked up, and land between the canal and the railway station was once covered in freight yards.

For a time, waterways and railways worked in tandem. Canal extensions were cut to take boats right into the railway depots to deliver building materials for the new warehouses and railway stations, and goods were transferred by crane directly from boat to train. But speedy, cheap rail freight ultimately put an end to the waterways. Only 17 years after the Regent's Canal was completed, the first mainline railway station was opened at Euston, and over the following decades the rail network took over throughout the country, often following the courses of the old canals.

There's a lot of new development on the next stretch, with a landscaped waterfront walk and stepped alfresco seating covered with bright green fake turf (things can only get better). As the canal curves gently round to the right, on the far bank, there's real greenery in the form of the Wildlife Trust's Camley Street Natural Park, an example of how a former coal depot and waste dump can be transformed into a delightful nature reserve; access to it, though, is via York Way and Goods Way. St Pancras Lock and Basin follow. In its industrial past, the Basin was a coal wharf and housed overhead tipping chutes from which waste cinders from steam trains were tipped into the barges beneath. Look across the lock to a quirky redbrick Victorian folly – an 1870s water tower that provided water for steam trains. It got in the way of the high-speed rail link to the Channel Tunnel, and had to be moved piecemeal then reconstructed in its present position. Overlooking the canal from the right is Gasometer No. 8, which was dismantled in 2011 and transported to Yorkshire for restoration then returned to its original position to be transformed into a park and event space.

A series of bridges heralds the approach to the first of a procession of locks at Camden. Between the double lock of Hampstead Road top lock and Limehouse Basin (see p. 28, *Short Cuts to Limehouse* walk), a total of 12 locks regulates the water levels over a drop of 86 feet (26m). Beneath Chalk Farm Road Bridge, look back to deeply-grooved black-painted iron uprights. Cast-iron strips were sometimes fixed to the vulnerable corners of bridges to protect against wet, gritty and abrasive tow-ropes. These at Camden, though, are the remains of a rolling mechanism that was designed to take the weight of the ropes, although the grooves suggest the system wasn't always effective. Pass the middle lock, and beneath an elegant iron footbridge. Take a break from the canal here to wander around the stalls and eateries of Camden Market, the site of a timber wharf until the 1960s. It was a resting spot for the canal horses, too: the former stables have been absorbed into Dingwalls club. There are also information centres for the Regent's Canal and Camden Lock.

From the market, return to the path, which humps over the entrance to a subterranean basin once occupied by a former gin warehouse. Ahead, beyond the next bridge, there is an odd folly of a building on the opposite bank. This is Pirate Castle, which was built in 1977 to allow local children to make the most of the water.

Pass under Prince Albert Bridge, and see that there seems to be another waterway coming up from the south. It is, however, Cumberland Basin, which was a servicing point for a nearby hay, meat and vegetable market until the beginning of the 20th century. Now the canal flows in a tunnel of peaceful green, beneath bridges with decorative, wrought-iron spandrels as it borders Regents Park. You can see the first of the elegant houses of the park's Outer Circle road. Not all are what they seem, however: the first porticoed and columned one is not 18th century at all but one of several villas in the neoclassical style designed in the early 2000s by architect Quinlan Terry.

Nash's Legacy

The need for a canal to bring coal and other essentials into the heart of London and through to the docklands coincided with architect John Nash's (1752–1835) plan for an upmarket garden estate. It was to be constructed on Henry VIII's former royal hunting ground of Marylebone Park. Nash, doyen of stuccoed Neo-classical Regency architecture (including the Mall and Buckingham Palace), also happened to be an investor in the canal. The waterway had to be incorporated into his plans for the Marylebone Estate and so he became its designer, with his assistant, James Morgan, as engineer. Nash originally saw the canal as a water feature cutting through the park, but it was decided that his elegant villas and terraces in their parkland setting and the industrial traffic of the canal were not a desirable mix. This is why the houses are raised atop high banks, so that the senses of Regency residents were not offended. It is also why the canal course is rather circuitous. The Prince Regent (later King George IV) gave his name to both the park and the new waterway. The later confusion of names – the stretch you have been walking is also seen as part of the Grand Union Canal – arises from the amalgamation of the Regent's Canal Company with the Grand Junction and

Opposite: *The Regency architect John Nash may have planned more than 50 elegant villas in his dream plan for the Marylebone Estate, but only eight were built. This Neo-classical gem is a late-20th-century design by architect Quinlan Terry.*

Warwick canal companies in 1929 to form the Grand Union Canal.

The wilderness of London Zoo interrupts residential grandeur for a while. Its original layout was designed in 1827 by Decimus Burton (1800–1881). The airy, aluminium-framed aviary, which was designed in 1961 by Anthony Armstrong-Jones (Lord Snowdon), soars above on the right like a network of trapezes and on the opposite bank are pens containing domesticated animals. Midway through the park borders, with cast-iron Doric-style columns, is Macclesfield Bridge, also known as Blow-up Bridge. It is a replica of the original, which was destroyed together with one barge, three men and a horse in 1874 when the barge's volatile cargo of loose sacks of gunpowder and barrels of petroleum exploded.

The next apparent bridge is particularly interesting, for it is in

Camden Market

Regent's Canal Information Centre

Prince Albert Road

Avenue Rd

London Zoo

Macclesfield Bridge

Regent's Park

Wellington Rd

Park Rd

Aberdeen Place

St John's Wood Rd

Lisson Grove

Maida Vale

Maida Hill Tunnel

N

British Waterways Office

Little Venice

Warwick Avenue

Blomfield Road

Maida Avenue

Edgware

500m (549 yards)

Blomfield Road

Delamere Terrace

Westbourne Terrace

Westbourne Rd

Browning's Pool

Westway A40

Paddington Basin

South Wharf Rd

Praed Street

Eastbourne Ter

Paddington Underground and Railway Station

Hampstead Road Lock — Camden Town Railway Station
Hawley Lock
Pirate Castle
Camden Town Underground Station
Cumberland Basin
St Pancras Lock & Basin
Camley Street Natural Park
Maiden Lane Bridge — Battlebridge Basin
Canal Museum
King's Cross Underground and Railway Station

fact an aqueduct channelling the waters of a lost river, the Tyburn, which Nash diverted to fill the ornamental lake in Regent's Park. More houses grace our route, then the towpath passes beneath the railway line that terminates at Marylebone Station. Just beyond the railway bridge, leave the canal to go up a railed zigzag path signed 'Lisson Grove', which leads back over the canal. Turn right, looking down to the initial reason for the diversion – a moorings-only section where the canal has broadened: this was once a wharf from which goods were transferred to the station freight yards.

The path winds up to Lisson Grove, which you cross and turn right to bridge the canal again, then turn left to walk in front of a residential estate briefly, before kinking left-right into Aberdeen Place. The barge horses would also have had to leave the canal at this point, because of the 272-yard (250m) Maida Hill Tunnel (see p. 38, *Barges Go West* walk). Meanwhile the bargees lay on their backs and 'legged' their way along the canal—pushed the boat along by walking their legs against the tunnel roof.

Spoils of Tunnelling

The building of the tunnel is said to have wrecked Thomas Lord's plans for a cricket ground; Lord was compensated by the canal company in money as well as in spoil from the tunnel's excavation, which he laid on his cricket ground nearby. Continue to Edgware Road and cross it into tree-lined Blomfield Road, which borders the beginning of the houseboat moorings known as 'Little

Venice'. Just before the end of the road at Warwick Avenue Bridge, cut down to the towpath at a gateway in the black iron railings. Go under the bridge to arrive in Browning's Pool, the point at which the old Grand Junction Canal from the Midlands joined up with the new Regent's Canal. The poet Robert Browning (1812–89) lived in nearby Warwick Crescent, hence the basin's name. The cottage just before the bridge on the left was where tolls were levied.

Follow the northern rim of Browning's Pool to the next (Westbourne Road) bridge; there's more of Little Venice beyond. Cross the bridge to join the south rim of the basin, which heads along the narrow Paddington Basin to the eponymous station (clearly signed). Long before the railway station was built (under the direction of Isambard Kingdom Brunel), Paddington Basin was a thriving inland port and was the terminus of the Grand Junction Canal before the Regent's Canal extension to the London docklands was cut. The Grand Junction had made that first vital connection between the industrial areas of central England and the Thames upstream at Brentford (see pages 14–19, *Hay and Bricks* walk), and the Paddington Basin brought it closer to the heart of London.

GEORGIAN DOCK BOOM: WAPPING–WESTFERRY

Summary: This is one of the longer, more intensive walks in this book, and it is packed with trading and river history, so allow yourself plenty of time. You will encounter Elizabethan explorers, merchant adventurers and the trading giants behind the first massive dock-building programme of the 19th century, and you will skirt the seedy Limehouse of the Victorian era captured so vividly in the works of novelists Charles Dickens (1812–70) and Peter Ackroyd (b. 1949).

START:	Wapping Underground Station
FINISH:	Westferry DLR Station
DISTANCE:	4 miles (6.7km)
REFRESHMENTS:	Various pubs en route, Canary Wharf pier; Pepper Street; Harbour Exchange Square; West India Dock

There is a sense of the fluctuating fortunes throughout the history of this area, which you will see as you trace its evolution from salt-marsh to the thriving docks of the Georgian era and the regenerated Docklands of today. The walk enables you to get your bearings among the dazzling high-rises of Docklands, and to visualize the great docks of the Georgian era. For more details on the Wapping and Shadwell stretches of this walk, see pages 62–68, *Georgian Docks Revisited* walk.

Turn right on leaving Wapping station, where Marc Brunel's Thames Tunnel from Rotherhithe terminated on its completion in 1843 (see pages 100–10, *Wharves and Warehouses* walk). Follow the road as it curves left opposite New Crane Place, then right along Wapping Wall, which marks the course of a former defence against flooding from the tidal Thames. Continue past the 16th-century Prospect of Whitby pub ignoring signs to Thames Path, left, and continue to the red iron drawbridge, which once lifted to allow ships to enter Shadwell Basin (an entrance to the early 19th-century London Docks).

On the far side of the bridge, turn right down the narrow path by the tennis courts into the King Edward Memorial Park. Before the park was opened in 1922, this was an area of derelict factories and houses known as the 'brick fields'; from the 1880s it was also the home of Shadwell Fish Market, which was intended to take the pressure off Billingsgate but didn't.

Remembering the Great Adventurers

Stop for a while by the attractive circular building at the edge of the park, whose ornate ironwork and combination of red brick and white stone belie its function as a ventilation shaft for the Rotherhithe Road Tunnel (see pages 82–89, *Surrey Side Up* walk). An inscribed tablet recalls pioneering adventure and England's quest to discover alternative trade routes to the southern seaways, which were dominated by the Spanish and Portuguese.

From the Thames shore before you, sailed Sir Hugh Willoughby, who was 'frozen unto death' while looking for a north-east passage in 1553; Stephen and William Borough, who were thwarted by ice and bad weather off the northernmost coast of Russia in 1556; and Martin Frobisher (1535–94), who made the first bid for the north-west passage 20 years later. Their ships had towering decks fore and aft and sails billowing from three masts, which was just one of many improvements introduced to ships in the 16th century. The extra masts could carry more complex and efficient rigging, hulls were more stable and the new, stern-mounted rudder increased manoeuvrability. The nearby village of Ratcliff became the victualling centre. The voyages of Willoughby *et al* opened up new opportunities, and over the following decades merchant adventurers formed new trade links; fur and wax came from Russia, while tobacco and sugar came from the New World of the Americas.

Continue along the Thames Path, past two multi-tiered stacks of red-brick apartments and the rather more elegant conversion of *c.*1795–6 warehouses at Free Trade Wharf. The wharf was built by the East India Company to handle its imports of saltpetre, which was used in gunpowder and to preserve meat. Dutch coasters were still calling at the wharf in the 1970s. The East India Company was founded in 1600 by London merchants who wanted to protect their trading interests in India and the Spice Islands of Indonesia. Over the two centuries that followed, the company became enormously influential in trade and industry, and thus in Britain's commerce and politics. In India it had its

Limehouse Basin
COMMERCIAL WAY
LIMEHOUSE CAUSEWAY
GRENADE ST
THREE COLTS
Westferry DLR Station
WEST INDIA DOCK ROAD
Salvation Army
Dockmaster's House
Museum in Docklands
ASPEN WAY
Paper Mill Wharf
The Grapes
Molines Wharf
Duke Shore Warehouse
Dunbar Wharf
MILLIGAN ST
WESTFERRY ROAD
GARFORD STREET
HERTSMERE RD
West India Quay DLR Station
Adam Place
Fisherman's Walk
Cannon Workshops
NTH COLONNADE
CANADA
DLR
STH COLONNADE
SQUARE
Canary Wharf Pier
Canary Wharf DLR Station
Canary Wharf Underground Station
No. 1 Gate
N
Limekiln Wharf/Limehouse Lock
Cascades
Jubilee Park
Heron Quays DLR Station
South Dock
ADMIRALS WAY
South Quay DLR Station
South Quay Plaza
Harbour Exchange Square
500m (549 yards)
Anchorage Point
CUBA ST
MARSH WALL
WESTFERRY ROAD
BYNG ST
STRAFFORD ST
MASTMAKER ST
MILLHARBOUR
River Thames
Isle of Dogs
Millwall Inner Dock
London Arena
Sir John McDougall Gardens
PEPPER ST
Crossharbour DLR Station
Printing Works
Glengall Bridge
GREENWICH VIEW PLACE
Millwall Outer Dock
Isle of Dogs Sailing Club

own army, and subjugated local rajahs until it was in control of much of the country. East India Company ships that traded in the pirate-ridden South China Sea were armed like naval vessels. For 200 years, the company had a monopoly on valuable goods from the Far East, such as silk, muslin, tea, spices and china. Back in London, the company's influence was evident on both sides of the Thames, where the company built wharves, warehouses, housing for its employees and shipbuilding and repair yards which turned out vessels at the cutting edge of marine technology.

Dickens's Territory

The path heads inland for a stretch to follow Narrow Street, which is lined with warehouses. Turn right down the path at the end of Sun Wharf and then go left to The Narrow pub. It is only a brief stretch of riverside path, but the views over the sweep of water round the 'nose' of the Isle of Dogs and the high-rises of Docklands are impressive. You get an idea of how much the peninsula added to a journey's length.

From the pub – a converted dockmaster's house (see pages 28–37, *Short Cuts to Limehouse* walk) – go up some steps and turn right across the entrance to Limehouse Basin. Continue past Papermill Wharf and another rash of converted warehouses, which bear no sign of supporting any sense of community life. Suddenly, you find yourself in a riverside development of an earlier time, with a terrace of houses with the distinctive, shallow-set windows of early Georgian style. The artist J.M.W. Turner (1775–1851) is among those who were inspired by this architectural enclave. It was certainly a haunt of the Victorian writer Charles Dickens, who in *Our Mutual Friend* (1866), describes the 16th-century Grapes pub (the 'Six Jolly Fellowship Porters' of the book) as 'a red-curtained tavern that stood dropsically bulging over the causeway'. To sit on the pub's narrow riverside balcony at high tide is as good as being afloat. At one time, a ladder led straight from the balcony to thirsty watermen waiting beneath in their wherries and provided discreet access for stolen and smuggled goods. The pub's reputed custom of getting clients drunk then rowing them out into the river, throwing them overboard and recovering the bodies the next day to sell them for anatomy experiments has happily ceased.

On to the Isle of Dogs

Keep to the right of the leafy gravel square, with its iron sculpture by Jane Ackroyd of a herring gull standing on a coil of rope. Pass Molines Wharf, with its wall-mounted crane, and Duke Shore warehouse. 'Shore' is a corruption of the word 'sewer'. We know there was a pottery here in 1660, for the diarist Samuel Pepys (1633–1703) records visiting it. Turn right at the beginning of Dunbar Wharf, signed Canary Wharf and Island Gardens, through the modern residential buildings. The curving tubular footbridge ahead takes you across Limekiln Wharf and on to the Isle of Dogs. This bulbous peninsula is formed by an enormous meander in the Thames. It was always isolated due to marshland to the north and the river to the south, but the Isle of Dogs became a true island when the Georgians launched their first major

Opposite: *The one-time entrance to the City Canal, which was opened in 1805 as a short-cut across the Isle of Dogs but never paid its way; you can still see the walls and chamber of the original lock. In 1929, the redbrick Pumping House was built to maintain water levels in the docks beyond, now dominated by the commercial centre of Canary Wharf.*

dock-building programme in the early 19th century. It apparently owes its name to the fact that King Henry VIII kept kennels for his hunting dogs there.

Cross the entrance to Limekiln Wharf, with its tasteful warehouse conversions that retain some original features. Lime kilns were introduced to this area in the 14th century and provided an essential ingredient for building mortar. The nearby

Sweet chestnut

Limehouse Pottery opened in the 1740s and led the field in producing England's first blue-and-white soft-paste porcelain in a bid to emulate the fine porcelain that was being shipped from China by the East India Company.

Walk beneath the skeletal tower extension to the block of flats ahead. Just behind the building is Milligan Street, named for wealthy Jamaican sugar-plantation owner, West India merchant and shipowner Robert Milligan (1746–1809), who was one of the founders of West India Dock (which we visit at the end of this walk). Canary Wharf Pier lies ahead, with its wide terrace, bars and restaurants. Continue straight ahead over Pumping Station Inlet and Limehouse Lock, the former entrance to the City Canal. Dangerous tidal waters and obsolete pumps are being tamed by 'a concrete raft foundation slab' to the level of Westferry Road, and will presumably support yet more riverside buildings. Tides here have always been a problem: in the 15th century, floods broke down the embankment wall at this spot. When they receded, a 5-acre (2-hectare) inland lake was left behind; it became known as the Poplar Gut and was a busy fishing spot; later, the Gut disappeared under the waters of the West India docks. The embankment was rebuilt further inland and the shore became a temporary storage place for stacks of timber. In the 18th and 19th centuries, the scene was dominated by busy shipbuilding yards.

The Millers' Tale

On the far side of the inlet, past West India Pier, look over the river and see where landmark skyscrapers such as The Shard, the Cheesegrater (Leadenhall Building) *et al* are in relation to the river. Soon, there's a welcome break in the riverside residences at the undulating green of Sir John McDougall Gardens, with mature chestnut and plane trees, while across the river lie Surrey Docks (see *Surrey Side Up* walk, p. 82). Now, in this south-west corner of the Isle of Dogs, you are in Millwall, whose name comes from the group of windmills which stood atop the wide tidal embankment that followed the river between Blackwall and Limehouse. The mills powered corn- and oilseed-grinding machinery, but were made redundant by the coming of steam power. The grain business in Millwall continued to flourish, however, and in 1868 Millwall Dock was opened to provide quays for on-the-spot unloading and processing of grain and timber.

Very soon after the park, take a left turn from the riverside path, which is blocked ahead by a serious brick wall. Reach Westferry Road and head right until you pass a works entrance (opposite Wateridge Close). Immediately after, turn left along a part-hidden, brick-walled and paved path, to walk beneath the towering iron gantries that once supported overhead cranes. The far side of the dock is flanked by monotonous yellow-brick residences, but our route is alleviated by the home of the Isle of Dogs Sailing Club, young plane trees and a chimney at the far end of the dock, which is all that remains of a former factory.

Follow the path to the left beneath two more gantries alongside Millwall Outer Dock, at the far end of which some Thames sailing barges might be moored. Millwall Dock was dominated in the 19th century and well into the 20th (when four pneumatic elevators, a 13-storey granary and silos lined the quays) by the mills of the McDougall family, who were pioneers of self-raising flour. The McDougalls had originally been involved in chemical fertilizers, but when Manchester chemist Alexander McDougall introduced a revolutionary new baking powder, his sons decided to focus on flour-milling. McDougall's mill operated here for nearly 100 years and was a major local employer; it closed in 1982 and was demolished soon after.

Glimpses of the Docks
Turn right into Pepper Street over Glengall Bridge, then left past a floating Chinese restaurant, along the right-hand side of Millwall Inner Dock, where dazzling glass buildings rise above black rectangles of water, to a string of shops, sandwich bars and estate agents, and Harbour Exchange Square. Reach the road at South Quay DLR Station, and cross over. The aim here is to get to South Dock, but redevelopment is happening, so follow diversions to the waterside and turn left. Then look right to a surprise vista of the Millennium Dome (now known as The O2 Arena) at Greenwich, which really confuses your sense of direction, as it's on the opposite side of the river. Continue along the dockside, and turn right over the steel-hawser suspension footbridge to Canary Wharf. Look left to the far end of the dock, beyond the modern buildings, to catch a glimpse of the 1929 pumping station by the now defunct City Canal, which you passed in front of at the beginning of the walk. The canal, funded by the Corporation of London and built between 1800 and 1805, seemed like a good idea as it cut across the Isle of Dogs, saving the 3-mile (5-km) round trip by river. It was never much used by ordinary shipping, though, and was sold to the West India Company, which, by 1802, had its own access via new docks just to the north. The canal was subsumed into South Dock, which dealt primarily in timber from the Baltic.

From the suspension bridge, go through the atrium of the building opposite and emerge into Jubilee Place; go straight across until just before the glass arch of Canary Wharf Station, turn right into Jubilee Park where water cascades down stepped slabs of grey stone. Turn left at the top to go along Upper Bank Street and take the second left into Canada Square, with its gleaming towers. At the steel columns of North Colonnade, turn left and then right to go through a shopping mall, and then follow the waterside left along Fisherman's Walk to reach West India Import Dock, the first of the great

Georgian docks, which was built in 1802. At Cabot Square, cross the footbridge to the north side of the quay and turn left. The Docklands Museum is housed in the warehouses on the right. In the water opposite, you may see a rare surviving example of a 'dirty British coaster with a salt-caked smoke stack', as immortalized by the poet John Masefield in 'Cargoes' (1903). Only two warehouses have survived on North Quay; originally there were nine, lining the waterside for half a mile (835m), to form the largest brick building in the world at the time.

An Overworked River

In the late 18th century, new trade routes had led to an increase in shipping, and the ships themselves were increasing in size. Vessels from all over the world were jostling for space on the Thames. Customs failed to keep up and ships queued for weeks to have their cargo weighed and taxed at the overcrowded 'Legal Quays'; security and policing were non-existent and pilfering and corruption were rife. A group of merchants importing from the West Indies joined with plantation owners, ship owners, agents, bankers and Members of Parliament to pressurize the Government into taking notice of their interests. One outcome was the building of the West India Docks, which not only provided a constant level of deep water that could be maintained by locks, but also offered fortress-like security.

A Government promise of a 21-year monopoly on handling coffee, sugar, rum, pimento, cotton and mahogany from the West Indies lured investors, and William Jessop (who was also Chief Engineer on the Grand Junction Canal) was hired as the engineer. Thirty acres (12 hectares) of earth were dug out manually to a depth of 23 feet (7m) for the import dock alone. Wide quays meant that cargo could be discharged under the direction of stevedores – or lumpers, as they were known – direct from the ships to the transit sheds and from there to the warehouses behind. One part of the quay became known as Blood Alley because the workers frequently suffered cuts from carrying rough sacks of brutally sharp sugar cane.

For the first time, ships and cargo were secure behind the high walls that surrounded the whole complex, and there was a 6-foot (2-m) ditch along the outer wall and military-style security. Since 1929, water levels in the docks have been maintained by massive pumps in the impounding station at the west end of South Dock. The original machinery is still used each night, drawing 4 million tons of water into the docks each year – enough to fill them three times over.

The Museum in Docklands

Part of the surviving warehouses is given over to the Museum in Docklands.

For an evocative and informative insight into the history of the Thames, London's development as a port and life and work in the docklands this museum is an absolute must. There are reconstructions of a Legal Quay and a 'sailor town' of the 19th century, restored river craft and newsreel footage of historic moments, such as the devastating bombing of the area during the Second World War. By targeting the London docklands, which handled a quarter of the country's imports, the Germans aimed to paralyse London and the country as a whole. In September 1940, a sustained attack by Luftwaffe planes destroyed most of the West India warehouses. Fires fuelled by stocks of inflammable sugar and rubber burned for days on end. The toll on human lives in this area was one of the highest in London. Yet the docks continued to operate throughout the war.

From the museum, return to the dockside and turn right, then left to walk around the end of it, going under the white gateway, a replica of the original Hibbert Gate (named after former dock chairman George Hibbert). Turn right and right again into Hertsmere Road, opposite the Cannon Workshops. This 1824 building housed engineering workshops and stores, and is named after the small cannon that stood at its entrance. The little circular domed building in front, dating from 1803, was used by the dock police and the Government's Military Guard for storing arms. On the opposite side of the road you can see the defensive walls, complete with spikes and barred windows, of the old warehouses. The red-brick building with a colonnaded porch on the left is the former headquarters of the Port of London Authority's West India Docks police division. Gone were the days when lumpers might conceal tobacco, sugar and other booty in their voluminous, broad-hemmed canvas jackets, for at the gates they might be stopped by police from the dock's own company, customs, city or port authority.

The Demise of the Original Docklands

Take the next road left, where the stark walls of a new cinema cast a shadow over the elegant former Dockmaster's House, left, which was built as an excise office between 1807 and 1809, but is now a restaurant. In West India Dock's heyday, however, it overlooked the No. 1 Gate, where the Portland stone piers still stand. This is the point where hundreds of hopeful labourers would turn up for the daily 'call on' in the hope of work. The availability of work on the docks fluctuated because trade in such crops as sugar and tobacco was seasonal and ships' schedules were affected by weather conditions, so dock labourers were hired as needed. A massive increase in trade – sevenfold over the 19th century as a whole – led to the frantic building of warehouses and a great influx of workers, but in the 1880s and 1890s business slumped and there was an oversupply of both. Dock and trading companies, desperate to sell warehouse space and in stiff competition, drastically cut costs – and pay. Once, dock labourers might have been sure of a day's work, but now they were being hired by the half-day or even the hour. A strike to improve working conditions called in 1889 by the Dock Labour Union resulted in the hourly rate increasing from 4d to 5d, but the 'call on' system continued until 1960.

In 1975 the docks were running at a loss of £8 million, and they were closed down the following year. By the late 1970s, 10,000 jobs had been lost in Docklands as a whole, 60 per cent of the water and surrounding land lay empty, and 9,000 local residents left the area. Today, 20 years after the London Docklands Development Corporation began its regeneration programme, a very different sort of life has returned to the area, and international trade is now handled at deep-water berths downstream in the Thames Estuary.

Beyond the pillars of No. 1 Gate, behind a high hedge just before the bridge, is the 1888 Salvation Army Hostel, formerly a temperance hostel for Scandinavian sailors. When you meet the main road, turn sharp left, almost back on yourself, into what appears to be an unprepossessing terrace of modern houses. Just beyond them, however, is a row of delightful cottages built in 1819 for the West India Dock Company police. Turn right at the end of Garford Street for Westferry DLR Station, which you will see ahead.

GEORGIAN DOCKS REVISITED: ST KATHARINE DOCKS– SHADWELL BASIN

Summary: Discover the lost – and found – remains of the smaller Georgian docks of the early 19th century. Relive the story of Wapping and Shadwell as they evolved from fishing hamlets into overcrowded, seedy and unsafe areas haunted by sailors, boatbuilders and rope- and sack-makers and then into desirable residential districts for the well-heeled. Some stretches of this route are overshadowed by multi-storeyed 19th-century warehouses, but there are also glimpses of a broad reach of the Thames where the basins and canals are like reflective gems among the dense buildings.

START AND FINISH:	Tower Hill Underground and DLR Station
DISTANCE:	3^1/$_2$ miles (5.8km)
REFRESHMENTS:	Various cafés and the Dickens Inn at St Katharine Docks; plus other memorable pubs en route

From Tower Hill Station head downhill, following signs for the Tower of London via the pedestrian walkway that goes beneath the busy roads overhead. It's worth a brief detour left to see a section of the London Wall: a single, mighty fortification that once encircled the Roman and medieval cities. You can spot the difference between the Roman wall with its sandstone base and courses of red tiles, and the rough masonry of medieval times, when a further 21 feet (6.4m) was added.

The Last Georgian Dock
When you reach a junction of paths around the remains of a medieval sentry gate, turn left to border the Tower's moat gardens, which were once a defence system filled with Thames water. Go up the steps to cross and turn right along Tower Bridge Approach. Just before the bridge, go down the steps and turn left downstream, through a cluster of cafés at the foot of an enormous concrete hotel complex on your left and the Thames on your right. Enjoy the exuberance of David Wynne's 1973

statue, *Girl with a Dolphin*. Cross the swing bridge across the entrance channel that connects the three basins of St Katharine Docks to the Thames. In the elegant house in front of you lived the Dockmaster; tall windows afforded him an excellent view of boats as they approached along the Thames and entered the docks. The house dates, like the docks themselves, from the early 19th century and is typical of the Georgian Neo-classical style.

Follow the path left, then right at the red drawbridge. St Katharine Docks were designed by the Scottish engineer Thomas Telford, who designed more than a thousand bridges, including the suspension bridge over the Menai Strait. These were the last of the Georgian docks to be built – they opened in 1828 – and they are the closest to the commercial heart of the City. St Katharine Docks were purpose-built to take small ships and lighters, which transferred goods from vessels berthed at West India and East India docks further east. In their construction, more than 1,250 houses were cleared and 11,000 people displaced, together with the medieval church of St Katharine, which was founded originally by Queen Matilda in 1147, and for which the dock was named. But the docks' commercial success was short lived, as their capacity and entrance soon proved too small for the new steam and iron ships.

Ahead is the Dickens Inn, a former 18th-century brewery warehouse with Elizabethan-style galleries superimposed; but unless you're in need of a pub stop, turn right at Marble Quay – named after the goods it handled – cross Mews Street and turn left along St Katharine's Way. On the right, look up at the cranes on the loading doors of Miller's Wharf warehouses. Pass Alderman's Stairs, the first of many a tempting narrow passage leading to the river – and a dead-end. People gathered on the steps to hail passing clinker-built wherries. Short-haul wherries were manned by a single waterman and those for longer trips by two; cries of 'Eastward ho!' or 'Westward ho!' indicated the wherry's direction.

Historic High Street

Turn right just past the alley for a very short stretch of the Thames Path (signed), but worthwhile for views of the Shard and Tower Bridge. The riverside then becomes blocked by buildings, so the walk dips inland briefly and turns right into Wapping High Street. Look across the road at this point for a glimpse of Hermitage Basin, a tiny remnant of London Docks, before turning right into Hermitage Riverside Memorial Garden, which, with its dove of peace sculpture, was long campaigned for as a memorial to the people of London's East End who died in the Blitz. Thames barges may be moored on the river.

Historically, the fishing village of Wapping was isolated, hemmed in by marshy land to the north and the river to the south. According to the 16th-century historian John Stow, Wapping High Street was a 'filthy strait passage, with alleys of small tenements or cottages'. The area became increasingly overcrowded and insanitary as river traffic and its associated trade grew in the 18th and 19th centuries. Today, the mostly 19th-century warehouses have been given a modern makeover and provide smart riverside flats for City workers. Names such as Cinnabar, Java and Zanzibar recall their exotic past.

Beyond the Garden, the riverside walkway comes to a full stop and turns left at a rather splendid Georgian house, one of a pair built for dock officials, which graced either side of the 'Pierhead', the former entrance to London Docks. If you had been walking along Wapping High Street in the 19th century, you would now be passing London Docks on your left. Three times the size of St Katharine Docks, London Docks were excavated between 1801 and 1805, taking the place of glass and rope works, and market gardens. The enterprise was more successful than St Katharine, partly because of the docks' greater extent, but especially because they enjoyed a 21-year monopoly of trade in any tobacco, rice and wine that came from outside the East and West Indies. By 1967, however, London and St Katharine docks were operating at a loss of £1.25 million. London Docks closed, and Daniel Asher Alexander's fine 1804–5 multistorey warehouses, which were known as 'stacks' and lined the North Quay, were demolished.

Crime and Punishment

Just after the pierhead, it's worth popping into the Town of Ramsgate pub on the right to drink with the ghosts of such luminaries as Captain William Bligh (1754–1817) and Fletcher Christian (c.1764–c.1793) in their companionable days before the mutiny on the *Bounty* in 1787. The Irish adventurer and Civil War Parliamentarian Captain Thomas Blood (c.1618–80) was apprehended here in 1671, clutching the coronation crown of Charles II (flattened with a mallet to make it easier to hide), which he had stolen from the Tower of London.

The adjacent Wapping Old Stairs led to Execution Dock, where crowds gathered in the 17th and 18th centuries to watch the public executions of mutineers and pirates, including, in 1701, naval officer-turned-pirate Captain William Kidd. The hangings took place at low tide and the corpses were then tarred and transferred to a body-shaped cage of banded iron and suspended from a gibbet in the river, to be removed only after three tides had washed over them. The last execution here was in 1830. It was at Wapping Old Stairs, too, that the notorious Judge Jeffreys (1645–89), who condemned more than 300 Royalist rebels to death in his Bloody Assizes of 1685, was captured in his attempt to follow James II into exile via a collier bound for Hamburg. (He was taken to the Tower of London, where he died of kidney stones caused by heavy drinking.)

Later, in the 19th and 20th centuries, oranges and spices were unloaded on this stretch of the riverside. There are still locals here who remember dockers breaking open a crate of oranges each morning and throwing fruit to passing schoolchildren. And the first fuchsia arrived in England via somewhere in Wapping – thanks to a sailor who'd brought a plant back from the West Indies.

After the mellow brick warehouses, the white and blue of Wapping Police Station is rather a shock, but shortly after on the right, opposite the park, just beyond Aberdeen Wharf, is the more conservatively designed base of the oldest uniformed police force in the country. Today, the building houses the Marine Support Unit of the Metropolitan Police; the original river police force was set up in 1798 to deal with the pilfering and corruption that plagued cargo-laden vessels as they queued up at quays to be passed by Customs. Proposed by a magistrate named Patrick Colquhoun, the force was funded by a pressure group of West India merchants (more than half of all losses were sustained by the West India fleet) and the Government. The looting problem was tackled by appointing offical gangs of lumpers (stevedores) to unload the ships and police watermen patrolled the river in wooden rowing boats. Within a year, losses were cut by 80 per cent. Today's unit has a fleet of eleven inflatables, six patrol vessels, a command launch and two land vehicles equipped with inflatables that can be dispatched to local canals, and is concerned principally with drug importation, terrorism, recovering bodies from the Thames and advising leisure users. Just after the police station are the tall warehouses of King Henry's Wharf and Gun Wharves, which recall the 16th-century site of a foundry that made cannons for Henry VIII's navy.

Shadwell's Place in History

Go straight ahead at the junction, past Wapping Underground Station, and opposite the entrance to New Crane Place – a concentration of storage warehouses at the start of Wapping High Street – curve left, then turn right, into Wapping Wall, so called because it was built over a 1560s sea wall, which in turn replaced medieval flood defences destroyed by heavy tides. Follow the road round to the left, passing the 15th-century Prospect of Whitby, which claims to be London's oldest riverside pub. A board on the front of the building lists the various monarchs whose subjects the pub has served. Notable customers of the past included Samuel Pepys in the 17th century and Charles Dickens in the 19th century. The pub's name dates from the late 18th century, when a collier called the *Prospect* from the east-coast port of Whitby was supposedly moored alongside the pub. Nip down the adjacent alley: if the tide's out, you can go down to a stony beach and look back at the balconies and gallows. There's a fine view of Bermondsey and Rotherhithe waterfronts and the warehouses of Butler's Wharf on the opposite, Surrey side of the river, and of Tower Bridge and south-east towards Canary Wharf.

From the pub, follow the road round to the left, just past the 1891 red-brick building, a former London Hydraulic Power Company pumping station. Until 1977, this generated power for the local dock machinery and for commercial buildings in west and central London. Just after the bridge, turn left into Shadwell Basin and walk round its north side past St Paul's Church, known as the Captains' Church because so many sea captains lived or lodged locally in the 18th century. The names of 75 captains and their wives are in the burial register of 1725–95 and the church's founder was connected with the East India Company. The explorer Captain James Cook (1728–79) lived in Shadwell in the 1760s and his eldest son was baptized at St Paul's. The original building fell into disrepair and the church you see today dates from the 1820s.

Now you circuit the basin to the right. Long ago, a beach of gravel among the surrounding mudflats and marshes provided a good landing spot and ensured the village of Shadwell its place in history. A Roman watchtower was built by the shore in the late 3rd century AD as a defence against Saxon pirates, and 'Shade Well' (meaning shallow stream) is mentioned in early medieval records. During Elizabeth I's reign, it was still a fishing hamlet on the lane between the Tower of London and the Manor of Stepney, but with the growth of shipping and trade in the 17th and 18th centuries, the population swelled with sailors and other marine workers. There's another Shadwell in Virginia, USA, which was the

Opposite: *The local heron's favoured fishing spot is a relic of Georgian docklands — the western-most 'Hermitage' entrance to the 30-acre London Docks built 1719–1815. The fortress-like wall is all that remains of the high-level security boundary to the docks; the redbrick Port of London Authority building dates from 1905.*

birthplace of American president Thomas Jefferson (1743–1826) and named after his mother's birthplace of Shadwell, London.

Smokers' Corner

At the far end of the basin turn left and right to loop round the basin entrance, taking the lower path alongside the water channel. After a short distance, at the crosspaths in the park, go straight ahead on the bricked path, then continue alongside Wapping Wood Canal (signposted St Katharine Docks), whose existence and landscaping saves this strip of upmarket residential development from being completely soulless. In Victorian times this whole area was taken up by the 35 acres (14 hectares) of London Docks. It was surrounded by courtyards, alleys and the lodging houses of dock labourers, sack-makers and watermen and was overcrowded with poverty-stricken families who scraped their living from the waterside.

Suddenly, and surprisingly amid the relentlessly urban landscape of today, is the early 19-century Tobacco Dock Warehouse, with its magnificent windows, and timber and cast-iron framework; it was once part of a 5-acre (2-hectare) complex forming the north side of London Docks. Just beyond are two replicas of ships that delivered cargoes to London in the 18th and 19th centuries. The docks were also an important wine depot, with 18 acres (7.3 hectares) of vaults beneath the quays, and also stored enormous quantities of wool, spice and ivory.

Shortly after Tobacco Dock, the path turns sharp left; ignore the right turn and keep on until the junction, with some of the original dock wall on the opposite bank. Turn right and continue to steps leading to Hermitage Basin, one of the former dock's entrance basins and now surrounded by yet more desirable residences. Exit by the remains of the old dock gateways and walls and turn right into Thomas More Street and follow it round to the left. Opposite the superstore buildings on the right, take the entrance, left, to St Katharine Docks (signposted), and walk along the right of the dock basin until you reach the main entrance with model elephants on the piers of the gateway. No surprise, then, to see, on your left, Ivory House, once the centre of valuable ivory imports. Turn left just past this to pass beneath the fine clock tower, then right along an arcade of shops to the drawbridge and small round building, which is now a café. Turn right here to walk along the back of the hotel complex, past a historic boat collection that includes Thames barges. Leave the dock and turn right to retrace your steps along St Katharine's Way and the Tower moat path to Tower Hill Station.

BULK CARGO: MUDCHUTE AND ISLE OF DOGS EAST

Summary: A short walk with opportunities for lingering over some classic London riverside views – notably of Greenwich waterfront and of broad reaches of the Thames and its shores beyond Docklands and the City. In the parts where concentrated residential developments get a little tedious, the names of streets and districts evoke a sense of this area's more interesting past.

START AND FINISH:	Island Gardens DLR Station
DISTANCE:	3 miles (4.9km)
REFRESHMENTS:	Café at Island Gardens; the Ferry House pub and other pubs and shops in Westferry Road

Scan the river panorama from Island Gardens with a painterly eye, for it is the one on which the 18th-century Venetian artist Canaletto based his 1752 painting *Greenwich Hospital from the North Bank of the Thames*. The reality has not always been as appealing as Canaletto's painting, for this site was nothing more than a waste dump in the 19th century, and unwelcome debris would wash ashore in front of Greenwich Hospital on the opposite bank. It's not surprising, then, that the Admiralty, which took over the hospital for its Naval College, had the area cleared and the park created in 1895 to improve its outlook across the river.

Greenwich River Crossings

From Island Gardens DLR Station, where the Greenwich Foot Tunnel emerges from beneath its glass-domed, red-brick rotunda, turn left at the junction with Ferry Street and cross it obliquely, passing Johnson's Drawdock, left, and continue along the street that runs parallel with the Thames. From *c.*1850, Johnson's Drawdock was one of the few public slipways on the River Thames that could be used by local industries. Small coasters and barges berthed at high tide at drawdocks and unloaded their cargo on to waiting carts at low tide. The site was blocked by a scrapyard for a time until the 1980s, when public access was reinstated as part of the Docklands regeneration and landscaping programme.

Turn left off the road to go through black iron gates at the side of the Ferry House inn, walk through the car park to the riverside path and turn right. Across the river, on Greenwich Quay, the tea clipper *Cutty Sark* is in its dry dock. The early 19th-century Ferry House inn was once the boarding point for the Greenwich ferry; customers could continue drinking in the pub's tower until they saw the ferry arrive. There was probably an earlier hostelry on this site, one of a handful of buildings that existed on the southern part of the Isle of Dogs in the 18th century. The opening of Greenwich Foot Tunnel in 1905 – and of the Blackwall Tunnel to the north a few years earlier, in 1897 – served to make the ancient ferry crossings and the Greenwich watermen who operated them redundant. There were ferry services between Greenwich and the Isle of Dogs from at least 1450, initially only for foot passengers; in 1812, when Westferry Road was built, a horse-ferry service was introduced to carry goods, animals and vehicles. Greenwich watermen were appeased by being granted permission to continue carrying foot passengers.

The Colour Factory

The riverside walk opens to a broad boulevard with rows of plane trees. At a break in the line of trees, look right to the workshops of Burrells Wharf, where, not so long ago, pink-tinted pigeons roosted on the rooftops, their feathers coloured by smoke from The Colour Factory chimneys. The factory manufactured chemical colours until its closure in 1986. The first industries here, in the middle decades of the 19th century, were linked with shipbuilding, but over the following decades these declined. Burrells, who took over the site in 1888, were initially exporters of paints, chemicals, pharmaceutical drugs and oils; they later concentrated on producing paint, dyes and pigments and then, from 1943, focused on chemical colours.

Continue along the riverside, past the workshops until a sunken space filled with great timbers on your right marks the spot where Isambard Kingdom Brunel's *Great Eastern* was built; at low tide you can look over the wall to the river shore and see the ridges of the ship's launching ramp. This white elephant of a ship was never commercially viable, but she memorably laid the first transatlantic telegraph cable connecting Britain and America (see pages 90–99, *Reinventing the Landscape* walk). The wooden piles are thought to mark the 1858 launching site of the ship, which was the largest of its day, unmatched in size and strength for 40 years. The *Great Eastern* was a combination of sailing ship, screw and paddle steamer, able to carry 12,000 tons of coal (enough to reach Australia without refuelling), as well as 800 first-class and 3,000 second-class passengers, or 10,000 troops. She ran at a loss as a transatlantic passenger liner, and had a working life of only 16 years. Two thousand labourers had worked to build her and several were killed in the process; in the course of her construction, both the shipyard and the ship's first owner were bankrupted. At the end of it all, Brunel was a sick man;

Isle of Dogs

he died barely a year after the ship's launch and just 10 days after being photographed on its deck.

Cubitt's Mudchute

After passing the skeletal supports of the old shipyard at Great Eastern Pier, continue along the riverside, passing Napier Avenue and Bering Square. Turn inland at the 'Thames Path' sign, to go through a residential estate at Mast House Terrace to Westferry Road, the main road that follows the loop of the Isle. Turn left and continue along Westferry Road to the wedge of the Millwall slipway. Just before this, on the opposite side of the road, look for a yellow-brick wall that marks the entrance to Millwall Outer Dock (see *Georgian Docks Revisited*, p. 62) and take it to follow the length of the dockside to its sharp right turn. At the end of this cut, exit the dockside, turn left into Spindrift Avenue and follow round to Eastferry Road. Down to the right is a surprise enclave of Victorian houses that has survived in this area of relentless regeneration. You, however, go over the pedestrian crossing, through a black iron gate into Mudchute Park. Mudchute Park and DLR station are named after the spoil excavated from Millwall Dock in the 1860s, which was carried on chutes to 'settle' in this area. This south-east corner of the Isle of Dogs is known as Cubitt Town, as it was largely developed in the 1850s and 1860s by William Cubitt (1785–1861), sometime Sheriff of London and Middlesex. He was a master builder whose company laid out local streets, housing estates and shops for the predominantly Irish workforce escaping famine in their native country. On the right is the red-brick Docklands Community Centre, home of The Island History Trust, where there are over 5,000 photographs of life in the docks through the ages.

From the black iron gate, head up the to the uppermost of two cross-paths and turn right along the route of a railway that once carried the rope-laying machines of the nearby Globe Ropeworks (1881–1971). If you look back over the park, you can see another relic of the past: the Millwall Viaduct, which was constructed in 1872 and now carries a Docklands Light Railway line. Beneath the path on both sides are allotments, pigsties and paddocks, for you are walking above the 35-acre (14-hectare) Mudchute City Farm. At the end of the path, go right and follow the road through the farm to its exit in Pier Street. At the end turn right, cross Manchester Road and continue past residential estates named after such nautical luminaries as single-handed round-the-world sailors Frances Chichester (1901–72) and Chay Blyth (b. 1940). Turn left at Seyssel Street and, at Saunders Ness Road, cross to follow

Opposite: *The pair of slipways launched the* Great Eastern, *the largest ship in the world in 1858, and the first made almost entirely from metal. It was not launched on the first attempt, though, when thousands of spectators turned up to watch; the 12,000-tonne ship stuck fast on the wooden ramps and wasn't successfully launched until three months later.*

Riverside Walkway signs to the river. (Ness is derived from the French *nez* for 'nose', referring to the nose-shaped lie of the land.)

The name Saunders appears on a 16th-century map of the Isle of Dogs and the road itself follows the line of an ancient track, which topped the wide tidal embankment of earth, wood and stones. The track – a kind of early version of the Isle of Dogs Westferry/Manchester ring road, but with an uninterrupted view of the Greenwich and Blackwall Reaches – once followed the entire loop of the Isle of Dogs from Limehouse to Blackwall. The bank was constructed to protect the area, which was known until 1800 as Poplar Marsh or Stepney Marsh, from flooding at high tide; the land inside the loop was drained with open ditches and turned into pasture. Here are views of Blackwall Reach, the Greenwich peninsula and Greenwich itself. Dominant is the Greenwich Power Station, which dwarfs the white Gothic almshouses that sit beside it.

As part of his development of the area, Cubitt divided the foreshore here into lots where shipbuilders, repair works and timber wharves set up business at the river's edge, backed by brick fields and cement works. The embankment was raised and straightened so that wharves could be built and ships could be moored alongside. Over a hundred years later, in the 1960s and 1970s, industries were closing down and were eventually replaced with the housing estates you see today.

Soon the Riverside Walkway circuits Newcastle Drawdock, a low-tide unloading spot for barges. The path continues on the far side back to Island Gardens DLR Station.

ROYAL FAVOURITES: GREENWICH CIRCULAR

Summary: Rarely for this book, there's some hillwalking – over the rollercoasters of Greenwich Park for sweeping views of the Thames and Docklands. Greenwich, with its glorious royal past, also evokes key moments in navigation, exploration and naval history, with insights en route into the achievements of Sir Francis Drake, Captain James Cook and John Harrison, whose chronometer enabled accurate navigation at sea.

START & FINISH:	Maze Hill Railway Station
DISTANCE:	3 miles (5km)
REFRESHMENTS:	Greenwich town centre; Trafalgar Tavern; the Yacht

Turn right from Maze Hill Station and left and right to cross into Greenwich Park by the gate near the corner. Take the path that follows the walled boundary of the park. About halfway up the hill, look obliquely right to see a wide flight of steps set into the grassy slope, and head for these. The steps take you to the summit of 'Belov'd of thousands, One Tree Hill', apparently one of Elizabeth I's (1533–1603) favourite spots. The quotation comes from *The London Chronicle* of 1784 and is carved into the semicircle of benches that commands a view of docklands old and new, and the site of the temporary 23,000-seater stadium for Olympic equestrian events.

Retrace your steps from the hill and take the first fork right. At the intersection, just past a splendid avenue of sweet chestnuts marching down the steep grassy slopes to your left (topped by one with a trunk resembling twisted ship's cables), take the sharp right-hand path (signed Queen Elizabeth Oak). Follow it downhill and keep straight ahead at the next intersection. The oak, whose remains lie beside a healthy young tree, in fact, predates Elizabeth I and is believed to have been big and hollow enough to have been used as a lock-up in the 12th century. It finally died in the 1800s, but over the following decades was propped up by a framework of ivy until it finally collapsed in 1991.

Most of the trees in Greenwich Park were planted by King Charles II (1630–85), and there are Spanish chestnuts, oaks, limes and plane trees that date from his time.

Greenwich's Role in Naval History

From Queen Elizabeth Oak head uphill towards the Old Royal Observatory, which was founded in 1675 by Charles II for 'the finding out of the longitude of places for perfecting navigation and astronomy' and designed by Sir Christopher Wren. The hilltop statue near the observatory is of General James Wolfe (1727–59), a Greenwich man who led the English against the French up the Heights of Abraham in Quebec and died a hero's death there. The victory gave Britain possession of the former French colony.

The observatory, a planetarium and a museum of navigational instruments and timepieces are incorporated into Flamsteed House, which was named after the first Astronomer Royal. Correct your watch as you stand at zero longitude – the boundary between the eastern and western hemispheres and the point from which the world's time is calculated – in the courtyard of Flamsteed House. A prize was offered for the person who could come up with a reliable means of calculating longitude, so that time and distance calculations could establish exact position at sea. The solution was John Harrison's fourth chronometer, which was tested by explorer Captain James Cook on his second Pacific voyage of discovery and became his 'never-failing guide' to navigation. If you are at Flamsteed House at 1pm you can watch the ball on the observatory's weathervane drop, which was a visual time-check for mariners on the Thames to set their chronometers by.

From the museum, turn left down a steep path that leads to the cross-park route of The Avenue. Continue on to exit the park into King William Walk and go straight to junction with busy Nelson Road, and turn left. Cross the main Greenwich High Road to go down a narrow path to the right of St Alfege Church. Alfege was the 29th Archbishop of Canterbury, who was captured by Viking raiders and murdered on the site of this church in 1012. The present-day building was designed by Nicholas Hawksmoor (1661–1736), one-time clerk to Sir Christopher Wren and later a distinguished architect in his own right, and dates from 1714. It is also where General Wolfe was buried and General Gordon of Khartoum (1833–85) was baptized.

At the point where the path corners left, turn right into the graveyard-cum-park and head immediately right via tombstones to emerge into Bardsley Lane. When major building works are completed c. 2017, you'll be able to turn left here to the main road at the end of the lane. Until then, turn right, then left down a cobbled lane, and left again at the main road. Cross the road at the traffic lights and go left over the Deptford Creek, then turn right to go through a housing estate on the left of the creek towards the River Thames. Deptford –

Opposite: *The tea clipper* Cutty Sark *has been raised 10 feet (3.05m) to protect its keel and enable visitors to walk beneath the gleaming curve of the copper alloy hull. The original go-faster hull was encased in a similar metal alloy over an innovative iron framework that was more rigid and took up less valuable cargo space than the earlier wooden hulls.*

meaning 'deep ford' – is the mouth of one of London's almost-lost rivers, the Ravensbourne. Once the source of power for numerous corn mills, the riverside is now largely inaccessible and functions as a storm-relief sewer.

The Navy-building Town

Waterside residential development has opened up a short stretch of riverside walkway, which is cut short by the Royal Naval Yard further along. It was along this stretch of river that Henry VIII (1491–1547) founded the royal dockyard that established Deptford as a major shipping centre for over 300 years. Deptford was long known as the 'navy-building town', but over the centuries the docks were used less and less until they closed in 1869. They were replaced by a cattle market, though part of the area today, at Convoy's Wharf, is once again a working dock, with a 'ro-ro' (roll-on, roll-off with minimum red tape) facility for paper imports.

The Elizabethan adventurer Francis Drake (1540–96) moored the *Golden*

Hinde here in 1579, after his pioneering circumnavigation voyage that laid the foundations for the East India trade (see pages 51–61, *Georgian Dock Boom* walk). Drake was knighted on board by Queen Elizabeth I. The queen ordered that the ship be kept at Deptford 'as a memorial of national honour and imperial enterprise'. It eventually disintegrated, but a working replica can be seen near Southwark Bridge (see pages 100–10, *Wharves and Warehouses* walk). It was at Deptford, too, that the ship *Resolution* was fitted out for Captain Cook's remarkable voyages of the 1770s, during which he ventured on untried routes round the world, twice crossing the Antarctic Circle, and discovered South Georgia and the South Sandwich Islands in the southern Atlantic.

When you reach the open area by the Thames, look left to a statue, donated by Russia, of Peter the Great (1672–1725) with a dwarf. Such was the reputation of England's sea power that Peter, Tzar of all the Russias, visited Deptford for a few months in 1698 to study shipbuilding. His behaviour during his trip was rather less than great: he stayed at the nearby house of diarist John Evelyn (1620–76) and partied every night. Evelyn returned to find broken furniture, torn bedlinen and bullet holes in paintings that had been used for target practice; the once carefully tended lawn looked like a battlefield.

Retrace your steps to the draw-footbridge over the mouth of Deptford Creek to the waterside boulevard on the opposite side. (If the footbridge is raised for shipping to pass through, you could retrace your steps to the main road and turn left onto the waterside boulevard just after the road bridge.) Follow the boulevard as it meets the Thames; and continue to the domed entrance of the Greenwich Foot Tunnel. Designed by Sir Alexander Binnie, the tunnel replaced a horse-ferry service to and from the Isle of Dogs that had been running since 1676. When it opened in 1902, emerging via a twin entrance in Island Gardens (see *Bulk Cargo*, p. 69), it provided a handy cut through to the docklands for Greenwich labourers; now it's used by migrants to the high-rise commercial centre.

Clippers and Yachts

Today, there is not even a commemorative plaque to mark the small drydock just before the tunnel entrance, which was once dubbed the 'grave' of the yacht *Gipsy Moth IV*, in which Francis Chichester sailed single-handedly to Australia and back in 1966–7. The challenge was to see if a modern yacht could match the times achieved by the 19th-century racing clippers, such as the *Cutty Sark*. It fell some way short but, nevertheless, Chichester's was the fastest voyage ever made in a small vessel at that time: he covered 29,630 miles (47,482km) in 226 days. Francis was knighted by Queen Elizabeth II (b. 1926), with the same sword with which Elizabeth I had knighted Francis Drake at Deptford. The boat's condition deteriorated in its 'cement tomb', but underwent a £400,000 restoration and once again sailed around the world in 2005. She was sold to The Maritime Trust in Cowes for the sum of '£1 and a gin and tonic' and is still sailing.

Clippers were so called because they clipped time off given schedules. Even after the advent of steam power, products that did not deteriorate with travel, such as tea, continued to be carried in sailing ships. Different companies competed against each other to break the record for the shortest journeys, but speed was also a top priority for more practical reasons: the first consignment of the yearly crop of tea fetched high prices on the London market and won a bonus for the crew.

The 19th-century clipper, the *Cutty Sark*, floating on a life raft of smoked glass, fills the east end of the quay. For several years, it was enshrouded in scaffolding, following restoration works and a devastating fire in 2007. Fortunately, as restoration had already begun, 50 per cent of the ship's timbers had been removed for conservation and so escaped destruction by fire. In 1885 the *Cutty Sark* sailed from Australia to England via Cape Horn in 72 days, breaking the record for the fastest voyage. She was the last of the windjammers to carry tea from India and China and wool from Australia in the 19th century. Even as she was launched in 1869, the newly opened Suez Canal was threatening her future: steamships could cut through the canal, shortening the journey between Europe and India by 7,000 miles (11,690km). The clippers still had to sail round Africa, vulnerable to the vagaries of the wind. The *Cutty Sark* was rigged to squeeze every possible advantage out of the wind. More than 11 miles (18.4km) of ropes controlled 32,000 square feet (2,973 sq m) of canvas sail – equivalent to the area of 11 tennis courts. The ship's figurehead is Nonnie the Witch, a character from Robert Burns's poem 'Tam O'Shanter', dressed in her nightshirt-like 'cutty sark' or short blouse. This and many more figureheads are on display in the cavernous depths of 'dry dock' that have been created beneath the restored ship, together with a café.

Nautical Memorabilia

Given the nautical theme of this walk, it is worth visiting the National Maritime Museum, where you can immerse yourself in Britain's maritime history from Tudor times to the present. Sail through maps and manuscripts, ship models and paraphernalia, valuable memorabilia of naval heroes and explorers such as Captain Cook and Admiral Lord Nelson and gaze at portraits galore.

To visit the museum, go around the stern of the *Cutty Sark*, turn right at the end of the path and left into the main avenue of the former Royal Naval College. Turn right at the crossing of wide avenues, where vistas open up right and left. Continue to the main road and cross to the next parade of impressive buildings – the Queen's House, a perfectly balanced gem of Palladian architecture by Inigo Jones (1573–1652), which was completed in 1638 and is flanked by the museum.

The Palace of Placentia

To rejoin the route, walk back to the crossing of avenues in the former Royal Naval College, but continue straight ahead to the riverside, then turn right. Where the college now stands was the site of the splendid Royal Palace of Placentia that was loved by King Henry VIII and his daughter Elizabeth. It was where King Henry married Catherine of Aragon in 1509, and where their daughter, later Mary Tudor, was born, as was Elizabeth, daughter of Henry's next queen, Anne Boleyn. The palace was wrecked during the civil wars (1639–60) and fell into ruin. The joint Protestant monarchs William and Mary, who reigned from 1689, decided to found a hospital for seamen on the site. They hired three of the greatest architects of all time: Sir Christopher Wren, Nicholas Hawksmoor and Sir John Vanbrugh (1664–1726).

Tzar Peter the Great commented that the finished building – great blocks of Baroque architecture separated by courtyards to preserve the river views – was wasted on 'worn-out seamen' and more fitted to royalty. Queen Mary had hoped that wounded, sick or aged seamen would 'live safely moored' in the hospital, but the institution was damned in the 18th century for being harshly run; as one Captain Baillie commented in 1771, 'columns, colonnades and friezes ill accord with bully beef and sour beer mixed with water'. The punishment for the slightest misdemeanour was for the offender to wear his uniform inside out, exposing the bright yellow lining. The end of the Napoleonic Wars (1803–15) brought a decline in wounded sailors, and the hospital was finally closed in 1869. It was taken over by the Admiralty as a naval college and since the Navy left in 1998 it has been let by a charitable trust.

Whitebait Dinners

The riverside path leads to the Trafalgar Tavern, built in 1837, whose balconies and bow windows were inspired by the galleries of Elizabethan man-o'-war ships. The pub was fashionable with 19th-century politicians and literary figures enticed by its 'whitebait dinners' served with iced champagne. One such was Charles Dickens, who set the wedding feast in *Our Mutual Friend* here. In the high whitebait season (from April to August), the river below would be busy with fishermen from Lambeth, Rotherhithe and Greenwich in their rigged clinker-built 'peterboats'.

Turn left down a flagstoned alleyway at the back of the Trafalgar past the Yacht pub and a terrace of neat Georgian and modern houses, back to the riverside. On the right is the quirky Gothic Trinity Hospital, which has been home to a succession of local elderly retired gentlemen since 1617. On the wall opposite are engraved marks, which record exceptionally high tides of the past. When you reach a wall set with charming bas-relief tiles by Amanda Hinge that tell *A Thames Tale*, turn right to cross the Old Woolwich Road and Trafalgar Road and head up Maze Hill to return to the railway station.

SURREY SIDE UP: ROTHERHITHE PENINSULA

Summary: In the beginning, the Rotherhithe peninsula was low-lying and waterlogged. Rotherhithe itself was a fishing village and the rest of the land was of little use for farming and settlement. By the 18th century, shipyards lined much of the waterfront, and by the 19th century almost the entire peninsula was taken up with back-to-back dock basins. Today, much of what used to be known as the Surrey Commercial Docks has been reclaimed by urban planners. The result is a delightful and accessible mix, with enough remnants of former docklands to conjure up an impressively industrious past, some unexpected wilderness and a network of waterside paths.

START AND FINISH:	Rotherhithe Railway Station
DISTANCE:	4 miles (6.7km)
REFRESHMENTS:	Pubs in Rotherhithe Street and at Greenland Dock; shopping mall at Canada Water/Surrey Quays

Route of the Pilgrim Fathers

Turn left out of Rotherhithe Station and left again into Railway Avenue, passing the Brunel Museum and Marc Brunel's 1800 Thames Tunnel engine house on your left (see pages 100–10, *Wharves and Warehouses* walk). Turn right into Rotherhithe Street, opposite Tunnel Wharf, and turn left at a little Thames-side garden at Cumberland Wharf on to the Thames Path. There, overlooking the reach of the Thames from which the *Mayflower* sailed in 1620 with many Rotherhithe pilgrims on board, is a statue of a Pilgrim Father and his lad by Peter McLean. Let your imagination sail and steam through the centuries, picturing in turn Elizabethan galleons, top heavy and billowing of sail, streamlined clippers bound for the Far East and Australia, steamer packets taking passengers to Gravesend, Ramsgate, Dover, Boulogne and Ostend and coasters bringing in cargo from Ipswich, Yarmouth and Hull.

The stretch by the river is brief; all too soon, you are forced to return to Rotherhithe Street, but there's drama ahead in the form of the red-girdered bridge over the outlet of the Surrey Water dock. Before you cross it, look left to

King Edward
Memorial Park

River Thames

Sports Ground

The Pump House

Lavender Pond
& Nature Reserve

PAGEANT CRESCENT

ROTHERHITHE ST

Canada Wharf

ACORN WALK

Blacksmiths
Arms PH

Nelson House

Nelson Dock

Ventilation Shaft

ROTHERHITHE ST

ROTHERHITHE THE TUNNEL

SALTER ROAD

SALTER ROAD

MAHOGANY CLOSE

Thames Path

Cumberland Wharf

RAILWAY
AVENUE

SALTER ROAD

SWAN ST

ROTHERHITHE ST

BRUNEL RD

*Surrey
Water*

Bacon's
College

Tunnel
Wharf

Brunel
Engine
House

Rotherhithe
Railway Station

BRUNEL ROAD

TUNNEL APPROACH

POOLMANS ST

Ecological
Park

Stave
Hill

Russia Dock
Woodland

N

500m (549 yards)

Albion Channel

SURREY QUAYS RD

Canada Water
Underground
Station

*Canada
Water*

REDRIFF RD

REDRIFF RD

OMEGA GATE

FINLAND ST

Norway Cut

SOUTH SEA ST

River Thames

Surrey Quays
Shopping Centre

Greenland Dock

SWEDEN GATE WAY

ROPE ST

South Dock

REDRIFF RD

LOWER ROAD

Surrey Quays
Underground
Station

GREENLAND QUAY

PLOUGH WAY

Surrey Docks
Watersports
Centre

see the ornate circular red-brick building. Its twin is across the river in the King
Edward Memorial Park (see pages 51–61, *Georgian Dock Boom* walk), and they
are, in fact, ventilation shafts for the Rotherhithe Tunnel, completed in 1908
(not to be confused with Marc Brunel's Thames Tunnel, which runs a little
further upstream). The Rotherhithe Tunnel provides a handy road route to the
new Docklands, but the footpath is not recommended because of the traffic

noise and fumes. The tunnel's entrance, beneath a steel arch, is in Lower Road, Rotherhithe, and is marked by a section of the 'shield', a 30-foot (10-m) diameter cylinder which, powered by hydraulic jacks, was used to inch through the bedrock beneath the Thames.

Rounding the Loop

Cross the bridge and turn left at the big pub to walk past block after block of riverside apartments and around or across inlets, until you reach a dead-end at a six-storey yellow-brick warehouse conversion. Turn right back onto Rotherhithe Street opposite Lavender House; turn left, cross the road, and then turn right off it at Beatson Walk. Take the immediate left turn uphill to skirt two sides of a sports ground, then turn left into Salter Road. After a few yards, just before a pond, turn left, passing a small but beautiful nature reserve and the Pumphouse, which was created by the Port of London Authority in 1930 to maintain the water level in the local docks.

Go straight across the road and through the side gate of apartment blocks, then cross the footbridge over an outlet to the Thames (if the gate is closed, continue right, along Rotherhithe Road then turn left at the courtyard with the obelisk). Suddenly before you is a close-up of Canary Wharf and the Isle of Dogs on the other side of the Thames, for you have rounded a big meander in the river. Continue until the next converted warehouse blocks the route and you must return to the road and go left past the Blacksmith's Arms and the elegant mid-18th-century Nelson House. Nelson Dock was a pioneering shipyard, producing wooden sailing ships and later composite hulls of timber overlaying iron frames.

Opposite Nelson House take the path marked Acorn Walk. Kink immediately left and then right. Fork right and follow the path to an underpass with mosaic pictures. We are heading towards Russia Dock Woodland, which, as its name suggests, is a wildlife park created from a former dock. Following the closure of the Surrey Docks in 1970, 423 of the peninsula's 460 acres (186 hectares) of dockland were filled in. Carry on along the main path until circles of cobbles, and the second footbridge, then go left, following the sign to Greenland Park and Stave Hill, to pass through ponds bordered by rich woodland. Follow the second pond round to the right and just before the next bridge take a clear right turn and another right which leads to Stave Hill. This symmetrical, man-made hill, which resembles a prehistoric burial mound, has splendid views over the

Opposite: *Greenland Dock was named for the country of origin of the whalers who used it from the 1720s. Later it was London's main timber terminal, and in the early 19th century, when it was nearly doubled in size to 22.5 acres (9.1 ha) and 31 feet (9.4 m) deep, even ocean liners could berth there.*

sea of trees to the Isle of Dogs; in the opposite direction, pick out the London Eye and Tower Bridge.

A Graphic History Lesson

Resist going down the enticing poplar- and lime-lined avenue that leads from the hill; instead, retrace your steps back down the path you came up and turn right at the first asphalt junction. Turn right again at the next T-junction, then immediately left. The part-cobbled path has mooring bollards and sections of rail for the travelling cranes of yesteryear, and borders a grassy basin, once a rectangle of water thick with working boats. If you've completely lost your sense of direction by now, look down at the end of this stretch to see the points of the compass set into the ground, with its exciting and graphic evocation of trade and commerce past.

Cargoes of softwood and other timber travelled 1,203 miles (2,009km) from Leningrad in the Baltic Sea; tar, oil and tallow were imported from Gdansk, Poland, and wheat and dairy produce came 3,135 miles (5,235km) across the Atlantic from Montreal, Canada. The dock basins that handled the goods took the names of the countries or regions they traded with: Baltic (completed in 1809), Canada (1876) and Quebec (1926). In an attempt to combat stiff competition from the other London docks and the railways, the individual dock companies south of the river amalgamated to form the Surrey Commercial Dock Company in 1864. As with London's other docks, the Surrey docks were enclosed and secure, with access strictly limited to official workers. They were also custom-built to transfer goods from ship to quay and warehouse much more efficiently than was possible at riverside berths.

As you walk the length of the quay the contrast between industrial past and parkland present is dramatic. From the Compass, go straight ahead, and then follow the path right to an underpass, which is actually the bed of the canal lock link between Greenland and Russia Docks. You'll see the other end of what was the Surrey Canal on the far side of Greenland Dock, which you are just about to meet. The canal was constructed between 1802 and 1805, when it ran through countryside to link with the Thames at Rotherhithe, but it was swallowed up by the Greenland Dock enlargement of the 1890s.

The Last of the Surrey Commercial Docks

Beyond the underpass, follow the left-hand path to the north quay of Greenland Dock, the largest surviving remnant of Surrey Commercial Docks. Its watery rectangle is as it was following the 1890s enlargement of the original Howland Wet Dock. This was one of London's earliest enclosed commercial docks, built between 1696 and 1699 and capable of holding 120 sailing ships. It became the main berthing for Arctic whalers and was soon renamed Greenland Dock. The original dock predated the Georgian docks on the north bank of the Thames by a century, but it was not allowed to handle dutiable cargoes.

In the 19th century, Greenland Dock went on to become the main UK port for timber from Scandinavia and the Baltic countries; the Surrey Docks as a whole were the world's biggest timber importers. Great towers of stacked planks and logs rose in blocks along the quay, separated by what were known as the 'roadways', which also provided some sort of fire break. For more than a century, Canadian grain was also a staple import in Greenland Dock and in the 1930s more than 2 million tons of tinned food, bacon, cheese, butter and fruit from North America were imported every year. The closure of Greenland Dock accompanied the general demise of the Surrey Commercial Docks in 1970; the basins just weren't deep enough for the vessels that were now transporting timber and grain.

The apartment blocks that surround Greenland Dock are arguably no more attractive than the transit sheds, warehouses and giant cold stores that lined the quays before the Second World War (most of these were destroyed in the Blitz, sounding the death knell for the North American foodstuffs business), but at least today the dockside is open to the public.

The Ravages of War

Turn left at the Moby Dick pub to follow the northern edge of Greenland Dock, passing over the Norway Cut swing bridge and a huddle of old barges, tugs and steamers. Turn right at the end of the dock to go along South Sea Street; over to the left are the iron bridge and lock that mark the dock's gateway to the Thames. Over the bridge, turn right to walk along Rainbow and Swedish quays on the south side of the dock until you reach the Surrey Docks Watersports Centre, which you have to go around before rejoining the dockside at Greenland Quay.

All along the Thames estuary, the river and docklands were a primary target for the German air force. The Surrey Docks suffered more damage than any other British dock area. In September 1940, the entire 350,000-ton stock of timber was destroyed by fire in a single night; the flames could be seen 30 miles (50km) away. But the London docks kept going and contributed massively to the war effort. Here at South Dock – and at Russia Dock, too – concrete blocks each weighing 3,375 tons were constructed at breakneck speed to make the 2-mile (3.3-km) floating Mulberry harbour for the D-Day landings in Normandy in 1944. The finished harbour enclosed an area 70 times larger than Greenland Dock. Look to the right for Steel Yard Cut into Greenland Dock. Because the lock had been wrecked by bombs, the concrete blocks were towed through here to the Thames; maximum clearance was just 9½ inches (24cm).

Greenland Quay is set with dockland memorabilia, including a capstan and a jigger, which opened and closed lock gates, powered by high-pressure water

Broad-bodied chaser (above) and golden-ring dragonflies, as found in Lavender Pond and Nature Park.

pumped from a riverside engine house. At the end of Greenland Dock turn right, and imagine the towering V-shaped perspectives of Cunard White Star liners moored alongside. Turn left and go under the red iron-girt swing bridge to reach a path alongside a massive shopping mall. Turn right to walk the length of the mall and cross the car park to walk down the west bank of Canada Water. Look out for the evocative statue by Philip Bews of deal porters balancing their timber load.

Near the end of the road, look across left to the clock tower of the late Victorian dockmaster's house; in dramatic contrast is the airy glass structure of Canada Water Underground Station opposite. Turn right at the junction, then right again down a footpath over a corner of Canada Water. Just before the footbridge, turn left down Albion Channel. This is London's answer to Amsterdam, a narrow waterway that ribbons its way calmly through residential developments. Follow it all the way, past Surrey Water, until the red swing bridge over Rotherhithe Street that you encountered at the beginning of the walk and turn left to retrace your steps to the station.

REINVENTING THE LANDSCAPE: GREENWICH EAST– WOOLWICH

Summary: The destination is Woolwich, home of the Thames Flood Barrier and one of the first royal dockyards, via the flat bulge of the Greenwich Peninsula and the still sensational O2 Arena, the dome built for the dawn of the second millennium. This landscape has been reclaimed from despair more than once in its history, and after years of redevelopment that blocked access to the riverside, you can now walk, run or cycle alongside the Thames almost all the way from Greenwich to Woolwich – and a thrilling journey it is too. Even the remaining minor diversions through gravel and concrete works now expose interesting inside views of sand mountains and loading chutes. The creation of venues and back-up facilities for the 2012 London Olympics further helped the peninsula's metamorphosis from toxic wasteland to streamlined sports and leisure park, with state-of-the-art sculptures and an overhead cable car slung across the river. The wide avenue of Olympian Way now follows the course of Old Man Thames as it broadens into the approaching estuary and is more obviously at the mercy of wind and tide.

START:	Maze Hill Railway Station
FINISH:	Woolwich Dockyard Railway Station
DISTANCE:	5 miles (8.3km)
REFRESHMENTS:	Ballast Quay, Greenwich; O2 Arena and beyond on Olympian Way; Anchor & Hope Lane, Woolwichtown

Turn right from Maze Hill Railway Station, cross Trafalgar Road right and turn left into Lassell Street. Greenwich Power Station, the titanic building with a tower at each corner, which makes it resemble an upturned table, once provided power for the London tram system and now serves London Underground. Head for the riverside path at Ballast Quay, which retains vestiges of its cobbled 18th-century character and listed buildings, most notably, the Cutty Sark pub, which dates from at least the beginning of the 18th century, and a row of later 18th-century houses. The ballast handled from this quay was made up of river dredgings and sand and gravel from Blackheath, just inland from Greenwich.

Ballast was big business: it was a neat and profitable way of disposing of the spoil from dock excavation, and provided stability for vessels emptied of their cargo. The quay's business, and the collier traffic that plied the river between Limehouse Stairs and Blackwall Point at the tip of the Greenwich Peninsula, was monitored from the 1855 harbourmaster's office.

Working Wharves
Beyond the Cutty Sark pub, a cobbled lane turns to smart riverside avenue, which you follow left and right all the way to Enderby Wharf. The 'River Garden' frontage for smart apartment blocks has replaced a string of grubby but rather more atmospheric old wharves and jetties. Work is still in progress on the creation of an 'enhanced' riverside that promises to retain 'important historical elements'. I hope so, for this stretch of river was a bustling hub of history and geography, trade and technology from the 18th to 20th centuries. Lovell's Wharf, just beyond Ballast Quay, was handling 118,000 tons of non-ferrous metal until the 1980s. At Granite Wharf, barges unloaded great blocks of stone, including Portland and Purbeck stone from Dorset, to be dressed and worked for such fitting monuments as Admiralty Arch, the London base for British sea lords.

There was a boatyard with a boiler house and a floating dock at Piper's Wharf, where lighters and workhouse barges that ease the loads of bigger ships are still brought for repair. For years in the early 20th century, Piper's barges dominated Thames Barge Races.

The Enderby Legacy
Despite promises of enhancement, I fear that the ghosts of Enderby Wharf's rich and colourful past will be banished beneath yet more 'boutique homes'. The white house with its octagonal glass-dome, which was the Enderby family's power-base, will be preserved. The historical associations of Enderby's Wharf will also be retained and 'enhanced', but planning proposals are not yet finalized and scheduled. The wharf's history and name stem from the Enderby family, who by 1790 were managing a fleet of whaling boats from this quay. As for many merchant adventurers, exploration and the mapping of new areas were natural extensions of their business. Charles Enderby was a founding member of the Royal Geographical Society; there is an Enderby Land in Antarctica, and several parts of the continent are named after captains in the Enderby fleet. For Herman Melville (1818–91), writing in his whaling novel *Moby Dick* (1851), the family ranked in importance alongside 'the united royal houses of the Tudors and Bourbons in point of real historical interest'.

The Enderbys diversified into rope-making in the 1830s, and later specializations on this site were appropriately cable-loading machinery and

Blackwall Tunnel
Slice of Reality
Blackwall Point
Ordnance Wharf
Reach
Blackwall
OLYMPIAN WAY
O2 Arena
Quantum Cloud
DRAWDOCK RD
Bugsby's Reach
North Greenwich Underground Station
EDMUND HALLEY WAY
River Thames
Emirates Airline
Greenwich Yacht Club
Victoria Deepwater Terminal
JOHN HARRISON WAY
Greenwich Peninsula Ecology Park
MORDEN WHARF RD
TUNNEL AVE
N
Jetty
Enderby's Wharf
Pipers Wharf
MAURITIUS RD
BLACKWALL LANE
Granite Wharf
BALLAST QUAY
CHRISTCHURCH WAY
500m (549 yards)
Cutty Sark PH
BANNING ST
Lovell's Wharf
PELTON RD
LASSELL ST
Greenwich Power Station
TRAFALGAR ROAD
HAZEL HILL
Maze Hill Railway Station

telegraph cable production. The wharf's greatest moment in history came in 1865, when the transatlantic cable that made the first telegraph connection between Europe and America was loaded on to the only ship large enough to carry it, Isambard Kingdom Brunel's *Great Eastern* (see pages 69–74, *Bulk Cargo* walk). When the cable was laid on the ocean bed between Ireland and Newfoundland, five words a minute could be transmitted electronically (if the

Woolwich Reach — River Thames — View Café & Information Centre — Thames Flood Barrier — JOSEPH GARDENS — HARLINGER ST — Defiance Walk — Clocktower House — WARSPITE RD — Animal Clinic — RUSTON RD — ST — WESTMOOR ST — EASTMOOR ST — RIVERSIDE — ANCHOR & HOPE LANE — LOMBARD WALL — WOOLWICH — CHURCH — FRANCES ST — Woolwich Dockyard Railway Station — BELSON RD — Gardens — WOOLWICH ROAD

words were short!). Perhaps there will also be space in the new landscape for artefacts, such as the huge iron winch that held back the cable, or the 'repeater' that was placed at 35-mile (58.5-km) intervals along the line to boost the signal; today, enough words to fill a million copies of the Bible are transmitted every second. Hi-tech communication continues in Greenwich today: in 1980 the first submarine optical cable was developed by a Greenwich-based company.

Just north of Enderby's Wharf is Bay Wharf, which enjoyed its moment of glory in the Second World War when barges for the invasion of France were constructed there.

An Industrial Landscape
There's a brief bucolic surprise in the form of a magnificent weeping willow draped over a miniature beach before the industrial desert that follows. You are directed slightly inland (at the junction signed Blackwall Point and Thames

Path, turn left) to wander between fenced-off gravel works. The peninsula has a long industrial history, and work is still very much in progress with mountains of sand and gravel waiting to be transported on overhead chutes to fill the holds of moored ships. Return to the river at a wide quayside soft with windblown sand from the massive cement works.

The location of the former Victoria Deepwater Terminal is clearly indicated. Across the water is the east side of the Isle of Dogs (see *Bulk Cargo*, p. 69). In the Terminal's heyday, the crane-like arms of unloading derricks stretched over the water. Just inland from here was a factory that, in the early 20th century, churned out 20 miles (32km) of linoleum flooring a week. The occasional old wooden jetty remains: one is planted with mosses and stonecrops; another, once the scene of jostling cargo boats and coasters with all the accompanying human activity, is now a wildlife reserve on stilts. Plants such as sea aster, sea buckthorn, teasel and evening primrose have been transplanted from similarly exposed areas downriver.

Pass a redundant gasometer and the highest of fences, which encloses a golf driving range; suddenly the O2 dome is in full view, ahead right. Nearing the tip of the peninsula sits Ordnance Wharf, site of the first industrial development on this reclaimed marshland in the 1690s. Guns, rifles and thousands of barrels of gunpowder were distributed from here, but the site was closed on safety grounds in the 1760s. Now, just offshore, there is an art installation by Richard Wilson created from a vertical slice of an ocean-going sand dredger. It is a 15 per cent portion of the original ship, and cuts through bridge, poop deck, accommodation and engine room. We follow the river's course round Blackwall Point, past a propeller-like sign that stands astride the Greenwich Meridian (see pages 75–81, *Royal Favourites* walk).

The tip of Greenwich Peninsula is a prime spot for watching wildfowl, particularly species such as oystercatcher, shelduck, dunlin, redshank, cormorant, snipe and teal, as they commute along the river highway between feeding grounds. The tidal marshes on the foreshore are rich habitats for shrimps, crabs and other invertebrates. The river is relatively quiet and clean compared with days gone by: from the 17th century onwards the Blackwall Shipyard across the river was churning out ships from East Indiamen to tea clippers, including the first steam ship (the *City of Edinboro*) in 1821 and naval frigates. Ballast barges, small tankers and coal carriers plied between the estuary and strings of busy wharves, their cargoes dispatched to Greenwich peninsula's brick and cement factories. Far beneath your feet runs the Blackwall Tunnel – a vital

Opposite: *The steel-clad helmets of the Thames Barrier span a 570-yard (520m) section of the river. Electrohydraulic-powered gates inside are closed to stem the flow of upstream water, when a lethal combination of tidal surge, strong wind and heavy rainfall threaten to flood London.*

commuting facility for Kent-side labourers working in the Georgian and Victorian docks of the Isle of Dogs and Canning Town.

To the Dome and Beyond

You are now by-passing the Millennium Dome, reborn as O2, a multi-purpose leisure complex with arena, cinemas, restaurants and bowling alley. When it was built, it was the world's largest dome, with a circumference of over half a mile (835m) and a 95,650 square yard (80,000 sq m) roof. The remarkable fabric covering, that stretches over a network of steel hawsers supported by 12 masts, is just $^1/_8$ inch (1mm) thick.

Blackwall Reach gives way to Bugsby's Reach. Bugsby, it is conjectured, is a common American name, so the reach may have been named after a New World sailor or pirate. Bugsby's Hole, a tidal mudflat nearby, was the point where the bodies of pirates hanged at Execution Dock (see pages 62–68, *Georgian Docks Revisited* walk) on the far bank, were suspended in iron cages until three tides had washed over them.

Olympian Revival

River and landscape broaden and flatten, anticipating the meeting with the sea. It is hard to imagine now, that the man-made and manicured area through which we are passing was a miasmic, mosquito-ridden salt-marsh until, in the 17th century, Dutch engineers built walls and embankments on the river to curb flood tides. Their efforts, together with a 1625 drainage programme, made the salt-marsh habitable for the first time. Osiers and reeds were grown commercially for basket-making, and wildfowling and fishing were the main livelihoods. The 19th and 20th centuries brought a host of industrial sites that no one else would tolerate in their back yard: oil refineries, gas works, chemical plants and power stations, leaving a legacy of badly contaminated land. For much of the 20th century, this was the unhealthiest part of London, and local residents and workers had the highest level of industry-related illness in the country.

What was for years a desolate wasteland of abandoned factories has gradually filled in with new-build apartments and enterprises, although parts of the riverbank have been sensitively and ecologically landscaped. Beaches, salt-marsh terraces and mudflats are being protected and improved under the direction of the Environment Agency, and banks are stabilized naturally with waterside plants and reed beds. The wide boulevard of 'Olympian Way' is laid out with landscaped gardens and punctuated with sculptures, including the burnished bronze *Liberty Grip* by Gary Hume, and Antony Gormley's *Quantum Cloud*, a spiky steel net condensing into a 30-foot (10-m) human body, which is one of the UK's tallest sculptures.

Sea aster

Keeping the Sea at Bay

Redevelopment also brought improved transport systems – with River Bus Stations, and the cable car constructed at a cost of £60 million in 2010, which 'flies' up top 90 feet (30m) high on a 10-minute journey to the area occupied by the vast, early 20th-century Royal Docks. Detours around the Greenwich Yacht Club Marina and cement works are well signed. But before the dust and rusty overhead chutes, it's worth taking a right turn at the Yacht Club junction to explore the Ecology Park, four acres of wild freshwater habitat. Return to the eastward course of the Thames, where the Thames Flood Barrier is soon in sight, striding across the river. Emerge in Anchor and Hope Lane, where, if bad weather strikes, you may, like many a skipper of the past, be forced to anchor and hope that things improve at the well-named Anchor and Hope pub. The pub is also one of several to claim to be where 18th-century printmaker William Hogarth (1697–1764) sketched out his illustrated moral tale of the ill-fated idle apprentice, who ended up being hanged for highway robbery. Pass Riverside Gardens, where traces of a Roman fort and an Iron Age settlement have been discovered, and continue to the Thames Barrier, which, for a while at least, is intended to prevent a combination of north wind and surge tide that could cause devastating floods.

Much of London lies on a broad flood plain, 2 to 3 miles (3.3 to 5km) wide; parts of areas such as Rotherhithe and the Isle of Dogs are reclaimed marshland and actually lie below high-tide level. In 1242, flood water stretched 6 miles (10km) from Lambeth to beyond Elephant and Castle; in 1579 fish were seen in the flood water that lay in the Great Hall at Westminster Palace; and in 1953 over 300 people were drowned in floods along the Thames Estuary and the east coast. The threat of future floods increases all the time, as the south of England is gradually sinking, ice caps are melting and the water level is rising. In the worst-case scenario, a combination of northerly winds and surge tides could flood London's underground system and seriously contaminate the water supply; thousands of people would have to be evacuated and the capital would be paralysed. The Thames Flood Barrier's shelf-life expires in 2030. Until then, when a surge tide threatens, the 10 giant gates, each one around 65 feet (20m) high, are rotated from their normal position on the river bed to form a steel wall facing downriver to stem the incoming wall of water. Inside the gleaming stainless-steel helmets are the electro-hydraulic operating systems.

Henry VIII's Woolwich

Security has tightened around the Thames Barrier buildings, and they cannot be approached closely, so just short of the Barrier, turn inland and left past car parks. Follow signs to the Learning Centre if you want to go there. If not, turn right (signed Woolwich Ferry) before the Centre, at the eastern end of a pretty park of wild grasses and silver birch trees. At a road – with a 'noted stout house' (look just beneath the roof), now an animal welfare clinic, on the right – continue along green and pleasant path to the main Woolwich Road. Turn left and follow the main road to a roundabout, then take the second exit, Ruston Road, towards a big chimney and warehouses. When you reach these – a former boiler works and iron foundry – turn left, opposite, into a housing estate, built on the site of Woolwich Dockyard, which was founded in 1513 by King Henry VIII. At the junction, go straight across the road and a community garden, under the building and through an unlocked gate to the riverside.

Woolwich probably started off as a harbour and market for wool: this is what the Anglo-Saxon name signifies, just as Lambeth was possibly a 'lamb wharf', for animals being transported across the river from the grazing fields of Essex. Henry changed all that by deciding to build his new dockyards at Woolwich and Deptford instead of Portsmouth. They were closer to the armouries and labour supply of London and to the king's favourite palace at Greenwich. The establishment of the Royal Laboratory, later the Royal Arsenal, half a mile or so downstream in 1695 was even more convenient for complementary arms supplies, and the dockyard held its own for the next couple of centuries. In the 19th century, despite having the first plant for repairing ships' steam engines in a naval dockyard, it failed to keep up with technological advances, and eventually closed in 1869. Woolwich was also a garrison town, home of the Royal Artillery, but this too has now gone.

Turn right along the riverside path; across the water is the massive Tate & Lyle sugar refinery building. Turn right and continue along the riverside, up and over an iron folly of a footbridge. When you reach the cannons, turn right up the steps; keep right, then left to pass the 18th-century Clocktower House on the right. This was the former base of the Admiral-Superintendent of the dockyard, whose job was to make sure that Admiralty instructions were carried out. Exit through the old dockyard gates and cross the road to Woolwich Dockyard Railway Station, which you see ahead to the left.

WHARVES AND WAREHOUSES: ROTHERHITHE–TOWER OF LONDON

Summary: This walk reveals a cross-section of London's history as a port, starting at the former fishing village of Rotherhithe and passing through the slums and warehouses of Victorian times to the sites of the original Roman port of Londinium and of medieval trade. You get a sense of London's changing fortunes and the impact of foreign invasion through the ages and learn about lighters, Legal Quays and the role of warehouses in international trade. It is a boom-and-bust story, with periods of flourishing trade followed by decay and despair and, from the beginning of the third millennium, a new life and a new look.

START:	Rotherhithe Rail Station
FINISH:	Tower Hill Underground and DLR Station
DISTANCE:	3 miles (5km)
REFRESHMENTS:	St Mary Church Street, Rotherhithe; Hay's Galleria, Butlers Wharf

Pioneering Engineering

From Rotherhithe Station turn left and immediately left again into Railway Avenue, past the Brunel Museum, left. The yellow-brick building is the original engine house, which provided steam power for the construction of the revolutionary Thames Tunnel. This was built in 1843 by Marc Isambard Brunel, helped by his promising son, Isambard Kingdom. An exhibition inside the tunnel tells the story of its building. It was one of the first tunnels to be built under water and used a pioneering 80-ton tunnelling shield, which not only prevented the soft river-bed clays from caving in, but was divided into working cells from which the navvies could hack away at the rock face. Nevertheless, the tunnel claimed several lives through flooding and the leaking of dangerous gases and took 17 years to build. It was one of London's must-see sights for visiting dignitaries and within 24 hours of opening around 50,000 people had walked through it. Stalls were set up in recesses in the tunnel walls, but the damp and gloomy route was always unpleasant. In 1869 the East London Railway Company bought the tunnel and created a railway link between Rotherhithe and Wapping, making this one of the oldest sections of underground railway in the world.

Religious Associations

With your back to the engine house, go left along Rotherhithe Street, passing the Mayflower pub, right, named after the ship that was chartered in Rotherhithe by the Pilgrim Fathers to go to America in 1620. Many of the Pilgrims – a separatist Protestant sect escaping persecution – came from this area.

Opposite the Mayflower, turn left into the cobbled St Mary Church Street and then right along Tunnel Road, to pass the church on your right. (It is now possible to take a shortcut to the Thames-side walk by going straight ahead at the Mayflower, but you miss some interesting sights). The elegant church was designed by John James, an associate of the rather more famous Sir Christopher Wren, and completed in 1715. The style of the church's structural features and the skill involved in creating them indicate that the work was perhaps done by local shipwrights. The fact that the church is built on a plinth to protect it against flooding reminds us of the threat posed by the tidal Thames. Inside the church are wood carvings by master craftsman Grinling Gibbons (1648–1721). Nautical relics include an oak table and two bishop's chairs made of oak recycled from the warship *Téméraire*, which played a key part in the Battle of Trafalgar in 1815 against the French emperor Napoleon. There is also a commemorative plaque to Christopher Jones, captain of the *Mayflower*, who was buried here in 1622. The ill-fated Prince Lee Boo, prince of an Indonesian tribe, is commemorated here too. He was brought to England in 1783 by the captain of the packet ship *Antelope*. Lee Boo was a novelty in London and became something of a celebrity, but 13 months after his arrival he died of smallpox.

Across from the church, note the two painted plaster figures of schoolchildren above the door of St Mary Rotherhithe Free School, which was founded by local mariner Peter Hills in 1613 (though this building dates from the early 18th century). Adjoining is the village watch-house and fire-engine house, dating from 1821. Next right is Hope Wharf, which includes an early 19th-century granary with a hipped roof. Legal Quays, where customs officials checked incoming goods on which duty could be charged, were introduced in the Pool of London, downstream of London Bridge, in 1558 (see pages 151–60, *Bridging the Thames* walk). With increasing trade, however, they became overloaded with work, and many lower-value imported goods came to be handled at these sufferance wharves on the south bank and at St Katharine Docks.

Local History

Continue along Tunnel Road to The Ship pub, then turn sharp right and follow the trunk-like curve of Elephant Lane towards the river. Turn left to go undercover along the riverside path, which is flanked by a shiny red-brick wall. At King's Stairs Gardens, pass the last building standing at the end of Fulford Street – the former offices of Braithwaite and Dean, a firm of Thames lightermen. Like many of the barges that sailed the tidal Thames, lighters – vessels that 'lightened' the loads of bigger cargo ships – had flat, boxlike hulls that could hold a lot of cargo and 'take the ground' at low tide. Initially, they were rowed or steered, moving with the flow of tides and currents, but later they were towed by tugs. Lighters also evolved into sailing barges with large square sails. In the 18th century, small sails were added fore and aft to improve efficiency when sailing against the wind.

Next building on the right is the Angel pub, which, despite its run-down exterior, is full of character inside. It was founded in the 15th century by the monks of Bermondsey Priory to refresh passing pilgrims, but soon became a haunt of smugglers and pirates and a place where unfortunate drinkers might be press-ganged into crewing ships. Navigator and explorer Captain James Cook spent many hours here planning his trip to Australia.

This stretch of river bank was settled by Neolithic and Bronze Age people between two and three thousand years ago, and traces of a 3,500-year-old timber causeway that once led across the marshy Rotherhithe peninsula have also been discovered. Just past the Angel, there used to be a sculpture composition by Diane Gorvin called *Dr Salter's Daydream*, but it was stolen in 2011. Dr Salter and his wife dedicated their lives to the poor of Bermondsey, a commitment that led indirectly to the death of their daughter. The sculpture depicted Salter in happier times, waving to his daughter while the family cat sat on the sea wall.

Look to the left now and imagine the moated mansion that stood here 700 years ago. In the 14th and 15th centuries, the riverside lands of the south-east were scattered with the homes of many wealthy landowners and ecclesiastical dignitaries, and this was one of King Edward III's residences. Today, the course of the moat and a crumbling wall are all you can see, but there's a helpful plan of how the mansion looked. Continue along Bermondsey Wall East until a cluster of trees announces your arrival at Cherry Gardens. The view from here was the setting for British artist J.M.W. Turner's engraving of the warship *Téméraire*, which played a key role in the 1805 Battle of Trafalgar, on her final journey to a Rotherhithe breaker's yard.

Follow the Thames Path until you break away from the river by turning left into Fountain Green Square, with the Old Justice pub ahead, right along Bermondsey

Opposite: *The Billingsgate Fish Market halls of the 1870s, designed by Tower Bridge architect Horace Jones, and the 1817 Custom House to the right are overshadowed by high-rises of the Second Millennium, including the 'Walkie-Talkie' and the pointed 'Gherkin'.*

Adelaide House & PLA

Trinity House

Tower Hill Underground and DLR Station

St Magnus the Martyr

All Hallows by the Tower

Fishmongers' Hall

TRINITY SQ.

DLR

TOWER HILL

Old Billinggate Market

LOWER THAMES ST

Southwark Cathedral

Custom House

LWR THAMES ST

TOWER HILL

The Tower of London

Golden Hinde

CATHEDRAL ST

London Bridge Hospital

Sugar Quay

St Thomas's Tower

LONDON BRIDGE

St Olaf Stairs

Cottons Centre

Three Quays

WINCHESTER WALK

GREEN DRAGON COURT

Tower Millennium Pier

Traitors Gate

HMS *Belfast*

DUKE STREET HILL

St Olaf House

Hay's Galleria

TOWER BRIDGE

SOUTHWARK STREET

City Hall

BEDALE ST

London Bridge Underground and Railway Station

TOOLEY STREET

Anchor Brewhouse

Globe PH

Butlers Wharf

SHAD THAMES

BOROUGH HIGH STREET

HORSELEYDOWN LANE

N

St Saviour's Dock

BERM

MILL ST

500m (549 yards)

Wall East and left down Loftie Street. Turn right into Chambers Street, where new apartments have replaced the giant, windowless concrete blocks that were cold stores built in the 1930s. At the end, turn right to join Bermondsey Wall West and, when the road turns sharply left, cross to turn right along a narrow path signposted Riverside Walkway, St Saviour's Dock, behind the corrugated orange and white building that is China Wharf (designed by Piers Gough and completed in 1988). Turn left to rejoin the Thames Path and go over the suspension footbridge that crosses St Saviour's Dock, where the river slaps brown-grey and dense with mud. St Saviour's Dock was once the mouth of another lost river, the Neckinger; the tidal inlet to which it was reduced was the site of grain, pea and spice mills in the 19th century.

A Dickensian Scene
We are deep in Victorian warehouse territory here. Despite the opening of the big Georgian docks across the river, many riverside wharves on the south bank

survived, dealing with trade from around Britain's coast and with duty-paid foreign cargo, which was transferred from the docked ocean-going ships by lighters. To deal with this cargo – swollen by the booming international trade of the first half of the 19th century – merchant companies invested in more and more warehousing, much of it on the south bank. Look out for surviving features, such as wall-mounted crane jibs by the loading doors. Inside the warehouses were winches, capstans, treadwheels and hydraulic jiggers to transfer the cargo. The riverside here went under the names of Folly Ditch and Jacob's Island and was surrounded by stinking millstream ditches. It was overcrowded, poor, dirty, black with smoke and, according to Charles Dickens, populated by 'unemployed labourers... ballast-heavers, coal-whippers, brazen women, ragged children, and the raff and refuse of the river'. It was here that he wrote of the villain Bill Sikes falling to his death from a warehouse ruin in *Oliver Twist* (1837).

Across the bridge is Shad Thames, with its river frontage, the Design Museum and Butlers Wharf, which was once the largest concentration of Victorian warehouses on the Thames, extending 131 yards (120m) inland. Now there are café terraces, expensive apartments and offices, dramatic iron sculptures that evoke ships' anchors and propellers and a useful location map detailing what you can see across the river. In the 1850s, the combined effects of a relaxation in customs duties on many goods and the repeal of the Corn Laws brought about a boom in trade. Six- to eight-storey warehouses began to replace the old riverside wharves, some of which contained their own silos for the bulk storage of grain, while breweries had their own granaries in which to store barley.

Exotic Imports

Towards the end of the run of restaurants, turn left down Maggie Blake's Cause (named for a local activist who campaigned for access to the riverside in the 1990s), and turn right along the cobbled street of Shad Thames. The exotic names of buildings and streets – Cardamom, Cuba, Jamaica, Cinnamon – recall the cargoes once stored here. Look back at high-level walkways used to transfer goods from wharves to warehouses. At the end of Shad Thames, just before you pass under Tower Bridge, look right to the Anchor Brewhouse, where the Scotsman John Courage brewed his first 51 barrels of beer in 1789. The present building, which once was a combined boiler house, brewery and malt mill, was rebuilt in the 1890s; the brewery closed in 1981. Opposite is Horseleydown Lane, where the brewery's dray horses rested up.

Tower Bridge, completed in 1894, was designed by Sir Horace Jones, who was also the architect of Old Billingsgate Market, which you can see on the opposite bank of the river. The bridge's towers complement those of the Tower of London nearby. In its heyday, the bridge opened to let river traffic through up to 50 times each day; now it's about 900 times in a whole year.

Your route is now paved with smooth blue-grey limestone brick, courtesy of Foster and Partners, the architects responsible for the tilting glass hemisphere of City Hall. This is the headquarters of the Greater London Authority and office of the Mayor of London. Its shape and tilt expose the minimum surface area to the sun and stepped floors shade those beneath. Instead of expensive air conditioning, the building is cooled by a water cooling system that is fed by underground water drawn up through boreholes. Panoramic views are to be had from the top-floor walkway. Looking upriver towards London Bridge you can see another Foster construction: the 2003 Swiss Re building, popularly known (owing to its shape) as 'The Gherkin'.

Ships Ancient and Modern

The way ahead is obvious, past the battleship grey of HMS *Belfast,* a battle cruiser built for speed and manoeuvrability and the last big armoured ship in Britain's Royal Navy. She was launched in 1938, saw active service in the Second World War and was saved from the scrapyard to come under the jurisdiction of the Imperial War Museum. A striking comparison is to be had with the replica of the 16th-century *Golden Hinde* further along this route. Next comes the magnificent shopping mall of Hay's Galleria. Alexander Hay built up his business empire on this site from 1651. The warehouses of 1856–7 were built in the fashionable Italianate style. The Hay's Wharf Company was famed for the fleet of tea clippers that brought tea from India to its warehouses, but it also pioneered cold storage and brought shipments of butter from New Zealand. Peep inside for the spectacle of the high arched roofs and the giant iron sculpture *The Navigators* by David Kemp (1987), an eccentric and delightful confection of nautical instruments contained in the shape of a ship's bow.

Inside the glass-fronted atrium of the Cottons Centre (Cotton's Wharf that was) members of the public can sit beside tropical plants and fountains. Now serviced offices, the original warehouses were where a bale of jute notoriously caught fire in 1861. The resulting conflagration, the Tooley Street Fire, fuelled by cotton, spices, rags and oil, raged for two weeks and consumed many warehouses, including the buildings on the western side of Hay's Dock (now Hay's Galleria), which had been completed just four years before. Outside the Cottons Centre are helpful plans pinpointing what you can see across the river, including Old Billingsgate Market. The path passes beneath the frontage of London Bridge Hospital, which replaced 19th-century warehouses with their Doric-style pilasters and sweeping arches, and the Art Deco St Olaf House. Norseman King Olaf joined forces with the English King Ethelred to recapture the City of London from the Vikings in 1014.

Continue along the path past these two buildings and turn immediately left down St Olaf Stairs (there are no longer any stairs), signposted Tooley Street, Southwark Cathedral. Kink left to see London Bridge Station entrance opposite, and turn right to reach the main road (Borough High Street). Turn left, cross the road and turn right under a bridge beneath the railway to reach the edge of Borough Market, and Southwark Cathedral, right. This is the site of London's first-ever recorded vegetable market, which dated from the 11th century. The tradition continues with the bustling Borough Market every Saturday. Keeping the cathedral forecourt to your right, reach a cobbled section of lane and fork left to the *Golden Hinde*, which lies ahead. The ship is a replica of the square rigger that carried Sir Francis Drake around the world between 1577 and 1580, and has circumnavigated Britain and toured North American ports. The average height of the 16th-century crew was just 5 feet 4 inches (1.65m). The ship measures 120 feet (37m) in length, compared with HMS *Belfast*'s 613 feet (188m), and weighs 305 tons, compared with *Belfast*'s 91,000 tons. From the ship, retrace your steps and turn sharp left at the fork to pass in front of the cathedral. Just downstream from here are traces of the timber bridge built in AD 1000 by the Saxons (see pages 151–60, *Bridging the Thames* walk).

The Roman City

Just before the pedestrian tunnel, look for the means of crossing London Bridge on foot: an open staircase of stainless steel, with York stone treads that cantilevers over the river, is planned to replace the old enclosed steps. Soon after their AD 43 invasion, the Romans developed their new port around a gravel stretch on the otherwise silty shore, and built the first timber London Bridge, about 160 foot (50m) in span, across the shallowest crossing place, downstream of the present bridge. Londinium became an administrative centre for the northern Roman Empire and was the principal port for goods coming in from other parts of the Empire, such as olive oil from North Africa, wine from Italy and pottery from France; grain, cattle and hides, gold, silver, iron, pewter, hunting dogs, oysters and slaves were exported. When the Empire crumbled and the Romans left, trade declined slowly but surely, the port silted up and the wooden bridge collapsed. By AD 500, the once-thriving port town had been abandoned.

On the north bank, just on the upstream, west side of the bridge is Fishmongers' Hall (1831–5), designed by 28-year-old Henry Roberts on the site of a 2nd-century Roman quay and, since the 14th century, a meeting place for fishmongers. The route continues downstream, with signposted diversions until the cantilever bridge link to the riverside path is completed. Immediately on the east, downstream side of the bridge, is an Art Deco building with star motifs – Adelaide House. When it was built between 1921 and 1925, it was London's tallest commercial building and the first to have a mini-golf course on its roof! Behind the riverside buildings is the church of St Magnus the Martyr, where a well-seasoned wooden remnant of one of the Roman jetties can be seen. Near here, too, were Roman baths overlooking the river; some well-preserved remains have been excavated.

The Famous Fish Market

The fish connections continue: look at the lamp posts along this stretch of the river and at the weathervane on the building like a squat French chateau, the Old Billingsgate Market, which operated on this site from the early Middle Ages until 1982, when business moved east to the North Quay of the West India Docks on the Isle of Dogs. Billingsgate Quay was one of London's oldest and busiest docks. Traditionally, it had long been a landing place for fresh produce, as well as timber, coal and corn, although a 1698 Act of Parliament established it as London's principal fish market. Citrus fruit and onions from Spain and salt were also landed there and the old wharf was the main landing for coal; the now demolished Coal Exchange was situated a little further along. By the 16th century, Billingsgate had superseded London's other busy quay of Queenhithe (see page 158, *Bridging the Thames* walk), just a little upstream, in importance. It had the advantages of being downstream of London Bridge, having a deep, recessed harbour and proximity to the City. Billingsgate developed its own peculiarities of language, its own characters and dress and gained notoriety. 'Fish fags', 'Billingsgates' and 'fish-wives' were all terms inspired by the market's gin-toting, pipe-smoking, tough, loud and foul-mouthed women of Billingsgate.

The Billingsgate building you see today dates from 1875 and was designed by the Tower Bridge architect Sir Horace Jones. It comprised a wood and brick market hall, a gallery from which cured fish was sold and a vaulted basement for shellfish, shops and warehouses. The old fish market building was refurbished in 1989 by Richard Rogers.

Policing the River

The path is flanked by blue railings above a stretch of the river where, from at least the 13th century, boats drew up to have their cargo assessed for import duty. The present Custom House building on your left, with its magnificently long façade, dates only from 1812–17, however. It was the administrative heart of port business, controlling the registration of ships, import and export duties, policing and smuggling. Ships' captains came ashore to register their goods in the Long Room. Customs officials known as 'tide waiters' boarded incoming vessels downriver at Gravesend and accompanied them to their moorings; then 'landing waiters' took over and weighed, measured and assessed the cargoes. In the mid-16th century, 20 ocean-going vessels a week had to be processed and this one quay could not cope, so Legal Quays were set up along the north bank between London Bridge and the Tower of London to spread the load. Each quay specialized in particular goods, which are recalled in the names given to parts of this walk; Sugar Quay, though, is named after the Tate & Lyle sugar processing company that built its headquarters here in the 1970s. There is little left of its origins now, as development changes the river frontage to contemporary residential, but simultaneously opens up the Thames Path. There may still be brief, well-signposted diversions. Across the river, Victorian warehouse conversions are miniaturised against the scintillating, high-rise background of the 'Shard', the highest building to date in Europe, and companions.

The Medieval City

We are now at the heart of the medieval port of London. The early Saxons had based their port of Lundenwic (see pages 151–60, *Bridging the Thames* walk), farther upstream, in the area that now lies beneath Covent Garden and the Strand. From the late 9th century, the port's focus was back downriver, where the Romans had originally built Londinium and the first London Bridge. Between 1176 and 1209, the first stone London Bridge was constructed. The Norman Conquest opened up cross-Channel business opportunities, and trade – especially in fine-quality English wool – flourished. By the mid-14th century, London was Britain's largest port and the city's population was sustained by imports from around Britain and Europe – wheat and barley from upriver country towns, such as Henley, and fish from Rye and Great Yarmouth.

Shipwrights, coopers, fishmongers, mercers (dealers in cloth) and other craftsmen and traders banded together in associations called guilds to protect their interests.

Look across the river here to the high curving arch of Hay's Galleria: in medieval times, the view would have been dominated by granaries and breweries. You have to go round the Tower Millennium Pier by turning left. Ahead, up the hill, you can see the grey porticoed pile – adorned by a swarthy statue of the sea god Poseidon – of the Port of London Authority (PLA) buildings. The PLA was set up in 1909 to take over responsibility for the enclosed docks and the management of the river below Teddington Lock, in west London. Next to it is Trinity House, the 20th-century headquarters of a company formed by royal charter in 1514 to manage pilots, buoys and beacons in the Thames Estuary and to keep the waterways clear of silt. Trinity House was also granted exclusive rights to sell ballast dredged from the river, which was used to stabilize boats that had discharged their cargo.

The Tower of London

Now turn right towards the entrance to the Tower of London and right just past the Tower Shop to go through the black iron-gated entrance to the river frontage of the Tower of London. Many of the towers doubled as watergates, which allowed access and could be shut to keep the high-tide water under control. The main watergate, beneath St Thomas's Tower, is now called Traitors Gate. Edward I had apartments on the top floor in the 13th century and the lower part later housed a tide mill that operated the Tower's water supply. The heart of the Tower was built over 900 years ago by William the Conqueror (c.1027–87) to impress and intimidate both the English natives he had just conquered and the invading Danes. It has served through the centuries as a prison for enemies of the State, an armoury, the royal mint, a stronghold for the royal family in times of danger and a storage place for Crown treasures and records. The wharf was a landing place for royalty and foreign dignitaries, as well as for captives facing imprisonment or execution. Since the reign of Henry VIII, guns have been fired from here to mark national celebrations.

At the end of the Tower frontage, turn left up some steps on to Tower Bridge and walk inland to the end of the Victorian iron railings, then left down some steps to the landscaped area north of the Tower. Ahead you can see the copper spire of All Hallows by the Tower. Turn right at the roundabout round the medieval postern or gate tower – the eastern entrance to the medieval city – through the underpass and straight up the steps to Tower Hill Underground and DLR Station.

THE WORKING WANDLE: RIVER THAMES–MERTON ABBEY MILLS

Summary: The River Wandle is the most interesting of the London Thames tributaries, because it offers a unique record of industrial history that started long before the Industrial Revolution. Much of the Wandle survives above ground and you can follow it on foot along most of its course. The northern stretch, from the Thames to Merton Abbey Mills, is where most of the industry was focused. You can link to the following walk (pages 118–24, *The Country Wandle* walk) to follow the river to its source.

START:	Wandsworth Town Railway Station
FINISH:	Colliers Wood Underground Station
DISTANCE:	4^1/$_2$ miles (7.5km)
REFRESHMENTS:	Various pubs, cafés and shops in Wandsworth and Earlsfield; Merton Abbey Mills

The Wandle's drop over its course, from the flanks of the North Downs to the Thames, and its strong, even flow have made it useless for navigation, but great for water power, and it was one of the best rivers in England for driving mills. In addition, the Wandle was linked by the great artery of the Thames to the ever-hungry markets of London, and it neither flooded nor froze over in winter.

Harnessing the Tides

From the station, cross to turn right along the main street (Old York Road) to Swandon Way; cross, turn right and take first left into Smugglers Way, under the railway bridge. At the junction turn left and join the pedestrianized Causeway at the end of the road. The Causeway was once the road to the village square over the marshy delta of the Wandle. Before this area was drained and built up, it was a plain laced with the Wandle's many streams. From medieval times until the late 19th century, a nearby mill harnessed energy from the rise and fall of the tides and willow shoots or osiers were cut

111

for basket-making and thatching.
Just to the east – towards the centre of
London – ran a canal, which linked the
Thames to the 8-mile (13.4-km) Surrey Iron Railway,
which opened at the height of Wandsworth's industrial
prosperity in 1802–1803. The Surrey Iron Railway was the world's first public
railway company, in that anyone could use it to transport their goods as long
as they paid the requisite toll. Horses dragged laden wagons along brittle cast-
iron rails from a canal dock to Croydon.

There were already several flour mills on the River Wandle by the first
millennium. Gradually, many other industries and settlements were established
and the Wandle valley became a thriving commercial centre, reaching the peak
of its prosperity in the early 19th century. As local historian Dorian Gerhold
records, 'few other parishes in the country had such a range of industries as
Wandsworth'; in 1805, the Wandle was described as the hardest worked river in
the world. The mills were working the river to the limit, using its energy to
power industries as diverse as lavender and leather processing and the
production of beer, gunpowder, chocolate, textiles and paper.

Tracing the Wandle's Route
Cross the Wandle and turn left (signposted Wandsworth, Earlsfield) along the
west bank of the river, under a bridge, and pass the sluice gate over Bell House
Creek, where a bell is engraved with the words 'I am rung by the tides'.
Continue to Dornay Street and the Armoury pub; cross the main road (Armoury

Way) and turn left, crossing the river before turning right into Ram Street. In Wandsworth's agricultural prehistory, this area was the site of Ram Field. Later the street formed the border of the Surrey Iron Railway. Look left to see inset into the brick wall a plaque commemorating the Surrey Iron Railway, which once ran along the route of this street. Beneath is a pair of stone sleepers on which the iron rails were laid. The next corner is the site of Young's Ram Brewery, which is reported to have been sold to a huge Chinese property developer, and will be turned into housing, shops and a brewing museum. Commercial brewing is recorded as having taken place here since 1576, which makes this the longest-running brewery site in Britain. Young's Brewery is open to the public and inside you can see 19th-century beam engines, historic brewing equipment and, in the stables, heavy dray horses.

A Walk in the Park

500m (549 yards)

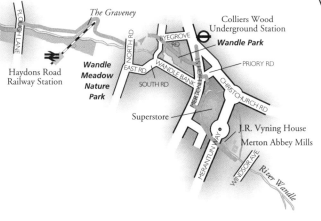

Turn right and cross Wandsworth High Street to head up Buckhold Road (signposted St George's Park 240yds). The river has disappeared beneath the former Arndale Centre, built in 1971 as the largest shopping mall in Europe and now revamped as Wandsworth Southside. Just after passing Southside loading bays, cross Neville Gill Close, turn left through the wrought-iron gateway into the park. The park, created in 1921, took the place of open fields and a rubbish dump. Pass the pond on the left, and follow the path round past the tennis courts. At the junction, turn left past a playground right, and leave the park beneath the wrought-iron arch, into Mapleton Road. After crossing a 1902 bridge over the Wandle, which has reappeared, turn right immediately down a brick-paved footpath above the river, back to the playing fields of St George's Park. Turn left past the sports field, towards the steps, and follow the park perimeter. An industrial estate echoes the Wandle's past, but once again the river disappears. Go straight across Kimber Road and along Foster's Way, still among playing fields. At a circular

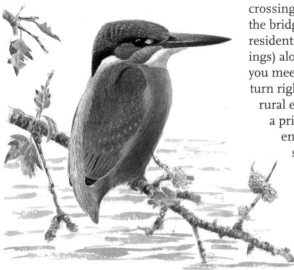

Kingfisher

crossing of paths, turn left across the bridge and walk through the residential estate (under the buildings) along St John's Drive until you meet busy Garratt Lane and turn right. Once one of many rural estate villages, Earlsfield is a prime example of the encroachment of London suburbia into the countryside, which was particularly rampant after the opening of the railway station in 1884.

A Legacy of Pollution

Pass the station on your left, turn right down Summerley Street and follow the road round to the left until you meet the river once more near the site – until junction with Trewint Street. Turn right to meet the river once more near the site of one of the gunpowder mills, which made Wandsworth England's second largest supplier of gunpowder in the late 17th century. Mill power was used to compress the potent mixture of saltpetre, charcoal and sulphur.

Cross the bridge and turn left down to the riverside path. Here, in the shadow of another industrial estate, this rural stretch may help you imagine the river as a once-famed trout stream, in spite of the odd shopping trolley and sundry rubbish. Pollution finally killed off the fish in the 19th century, but today there are once again a few hopeful fishermen, and riverside plants and birds find peace from the never-ending roar of suburban traffic. Pass beneath the pylons, past a power station and cross Plough Lane, turning left then right to continue on the riverside trail on the opposite bank. An iron walkway, right, marks where the river meets its only significant tributary, the Graveney, which flows, mainly below ground, from Tooting.

Beyond the railway bridge, at a junction of paths, turn right to the open land that is Wandle Meadow. There are a couple of rather clogged up ponds

Opposite: *The inscription on the bell hung above a sluice gate on the River Wandle at Bell Creek reads, 'I am rung by the tides', and ring it does, four times in every 24-hour period.*

to the right. Turn left along a gravel path, which leads across the meadow. Look out for rectangular indentations in the ground – traces of the former sewage works. This is a cared-for spot, where the locals have regular clean-up days and where kingfishers are known to ply the route from further upstream.

Messrs Nelson and Morris

The path wiggles right and through a tunnel beneath North Road, then heads diagonally over the next open space to join a small residential road. There's a former waterworks on the right; keep to the left of it and pass a terrace of modern houses. Cross the road to a gateway in the brick wall into Wandle Park. Follow any of the paths leading south through the park towards the fountain in the far left-hand corner. This pocket of natural beauty, where the Wandle has been nurtured into streams and wildlife ponds, was opened in 1907 and is now under the auspices of the National Trust. It was formerly the grounds of Wandle Bank House, one-time home of a friend and neighbour of Admiral Lord Nelson. The fountain is a relic from the grounds; pause a while to read the apt inscription at its base, a quotation from Matthew Arnold's 'Lines Written in Kensington Gardens', before you emerge to the 'city's jar' of Merton High Street.

Turn right and cross the road to the business estate opposite. It's hard to imagine that there were once commercial watercress beds here! Go to the right behind the first block of commercial buildings and turn left at the Pickle Ditch noticeboard (with restoration and nature notes) to follow the river. The hypermarket lies over the old site of Morris & Co., founded in 1881 by William Morris (1834–96), pioneer of the Arts and Crafts Movement and probably the most influential designer of the late 19th century. Morris abhorred the drudgery of mass production and wanted to recapture the simplicity and creativity of medieval craftsmanship. Many of his distinctive chintzes, tapestries and carpets were produced on this site, together with stained glass, and sold through the Regent Street department store Liberty, who printed their own famous fabrics at nearby Merton Abbey Mills.

Turn right across the footbridge at the hypermarket entrance and immediately left along a pretty wooded stretch of the Wandle. This area caught the attention of Emma, Lady Hamilton (c.1765–1815), mistress of Admiral Lord Nelson (1758–1805): in 1801 she bought the adjacent Merton estate to live with both her illustrious lover and her husband in a *ménage à trois*. The waters of the Wandle fed a canal that was cut through the grounds, which Emma called 'The Nile' and which she stocked with waterfowl and fish. The house was sold following Nelson's death in the Battle of Trafalgar in 1805 and the estate gradually broke up; it is remembered now only in local street names.

The path emerges into a small car park, which you cross to go through an archway, at whose base are stones from the medieval Merton Priory. In Emma Hamilton's day, Merton was still a small village which had built up around the priory. Cross Merantun Way, which traverses the now defunct line of the 1869 rail route that linked Wimbledon and Tooting via Merton Park and gave a boost to local industries; continue down the path signed Morden Hall Park. Across the river on the left is a superb example of Arts and Crafts architecture – a house designed by architect J.R. Vyning in 1912. You have now reached Merton Abbey Mills, where you can capture something of the atmosphere of the past. Here, old mill buildings have been turned into craft markets and ethnic food stalls and the Liberty factory's Victorian waterwheel has been restored. In the museum you will discover more about the mills' history and about William Morris and the Arts and Crafts Movement.

From Merton Abbey Mills, return across Merantun Way, and head for a riverside walk along the left-hand side of the 'superstore' complex. Keep right for Colliers Wood Underground Station.

THE COUNTRY WANDLE: MORDEN–WADDON PONDS

Summary: The route follows the Wandle through established parkland and snatches of countryside to one of its two present-day sources at Waddon Ponds. Explore the river's changing moods as it flows between concrete strait-jackets and rural meanders, bypasses industrial estates and the sites of former mills and factories. It flows through parkland, including Morden Hall and Beddington parks, which provides welcome relief from the surrounding suburbia.

START:	Morden Road Tramline Station
FINISH:	Waddon Railway Station
DISTANCE:	7 miles (11.7km)
REFRESHMENTS:	Morden Hall Park; Surrey Arms, Morden Road; the Palmerston pub, Mill Lane

From Morden Road Tramline Station, take the exit that crosses beneath Morden Road, go up the steps and turn left. Just past the advertising billboards turn left down the sandy gravelled track signed Phipps Bridge; continue until the track opens on to the water meadows, then take a clear right turn signed Morden Hall Park.

Modern Hall Park
The path through the 125-acre (50-hectare) park first winds through Wandle wetlands, which are managed to create a valuable habitat for wetland birds, such as herons, plants and insects. Just after a wooden bridge there's a junction with

Opposite: *The job of this waterwheel was to divert water from the River Wandle to power the millstones that ground tobacco leaves into powdered snuff, and it continued in this use until 1922.*

a blue signpost: turn left here and look right over another small bridge towards an ornamental aqueduct, weir, lake and Morden Hall itself. The park is now owned by the National Trust, but way back in Elizabethan times there were hay meadows here and, indeed, the grass is still cut for hay once a year. The park was planted by the Hatfield family, who made their fortune from snuff-milling; the house dates from *c*.1750.

Instead of crossing the white wrought-iron bridge, bear right of it to visit craft workshops and the Snuff Mill. Snuff (ground tobacco) superseded chewing tobacco from the early 18th century and was at its most popular during the reign of George IV (1820–30). You can see the kilns where the tobacco leaves were dried, a waterwheel on a channel that diverts water from the Wandle and the great millstones that ground the tobacco into a powder fine enough to sniff. The last snuff was milled here in 1922.

Leaving the snuff factory, turn right to walk past white Morden Cottage and a centuries-old yew tree and rejoin the main path through the park, turning right along an avenue of stately limes and chestnuts. Follow the avenue, which was planted in the 1870s, as it curves to the right, looking left to admire a splendid weeping beech tree and, on reaching Morden Road, turn right. There's a pub stop here at the Surrey Arms just to the left.

Ravensbury Park

Turn right and cross the road to rejoin the trail (signed Ravensbury Park) to the left just before the road crosses the river, then head immediately right through the gate in the railings. On the far bank is the site of Ravensbury Mill, partly replaced now by riverside housing. Ravensbury was reputedly the river's last working mill. It produced snuff from 1755 to 1925 and during the Second World War was adapted to generate electricity and was occasionally used to power woodworking machinery. The Ravensbury Park of today is a remnant of one of Mitcham's four medieval manors. From the late 17th century to c.1860, it was also a major player in the thriving local textile industry; towards the centre of the park there are traces of parallel watercourses, which were used for bleaching.

As you cross an iron-railed bridge to walk along the opposite bank of the river, straight ahead is a pair of millstones, now sadly defaced by graffiti, which were once turned by the horizontal cog wheel above. The path is lined by sturdy horse-chestnut trees, then on the left is one of the park's 200-year-old plane trees, with its impressive mottled trunk. The park is noted for its variety of trees. Keep straight ahead at the fork here, and follow the broad, attractive stretch of river, which is popular with waterfowl. Look in the tree canopy for flocks of green parakeets that have naturalized in London, and on the river itself for the less welcome invader, floating pennywort, with its buttercup-like leaves; this pest of a plant overwhelms anything in its path. Turn right over second iron-railed bridge, then left, passing some mature willows on the opposite bank, straight on at the next bridge, then veer round to the left over another bridge and past three-storey flats, before reaching London Road.

The Meandering Wandle

Turn right, cross the road, pass over the river and head left down the path for Watermeads and Poulter Park. Through the railings on the opposite bank you can glimpse white weatherboarded millworkers' cottages of the 18th and 19th centuries. Follow the iron railings until you reach a fork at the end of an all-weather sports field. Take the right-hand option. This leads to a delightful rural curve in the river beneath Bishopsford House. All too soon, however, an industrial estate rears up on the east bank. In summer the path is invaded by Japanese knotweed (which resists most attempts at being curbed), hogweed, nettles, dock and the giant leaves and spiky-balled seed heads of giant burdock.

Hogweed

Negotiate an iron gate, taking note of the Wandle's energetic flow as it tumbles round the corner, and pass alongside the terraced cottages of Watermead Lane. Turn right and cross Goat Road. The business park opposite was once a site for lavender and leather processing. Turn left immediately, passing a Georgian house across the river, left, and bear left, signposted Buckhurst Avenue, to follow the stream and blue-painted railings.

The next section is a bit grubby, with badly drained land to the right and occasional factory buildings on the left bank. The metalled path is flanked on the right by railings. At the footbridge, keep straight ahead to follow a short but slow and peaceful stretch of the river with suburban houses to the right; willowherb and yellow flag iris add summer colour. The closer you get to a rather run-down complex of flats, the less watercress there is in the river and the more rubbish. At the road, turn left then right down the residential cul-de-sac of Culvers Retreat, which is signposted Poulter Park. The continuation of the path is obvious on the left just before the housing ends.

Wilderness Island

Cross a little humpback bridge, where the dreaded floating pennywort has taken hold, and turn immediately right, heading towards the green-arched road bridge. Turn right over the bridge, cross the road and turn left to rejoin the Wandle. Pass a weir and a fine plane tree and continue along a metalled path. On your left, at the confluence of the two branches of the Wandle, is a nature reserve managed by the London Wildlife Trust and aptly named Wilderness Island. The entrance is off Mill Lane, into which the path leads. Turn left along the lane, where it is signposted Carshalton Ponds.

Now you have the option of saving about 20 minutes of walking by turning left along Butter Hill. The principal route, however, is to continue straight ahead along the east bank of the river through a housing estate alleviated by silver birches. Turn right to cross the river at the bridge with concrete spheres (the Palmerston pub is just up the road on the right) and proceed along the west bank. Turn left at the next bridge to walk through the gardens towards Carshalton Ponds, one of the two main sources of the Wandle. The waters that feed the Wandle originate in the North Downs but filter through the chalk and travel underground until they bubble up in a series of springs between the South London border towns of Croydon and Carshalton. There was a time when the river flowed through what is now the centre of Croydon, but it is now confined to pipes and the two main branches of the river now emerge from Carshalton and Waddon Ponds.

Beddington Park

Take the park path to the left, past the red-brick council offices, and, after passing the children's playground and sports courts, turn left at the signpost for Beddington Park. Turn right across the river to the Westcroft Leisure Centre and turn right, then left along Westcroft Road. At the end, turn left and, after the pond with a fountain, cross the busy London Road (if you have taken the Butter Hill short cut, pick up the route from this point), then turn left into Lakeside, with its row of ponds. Keep straight ahead along a flagstoned path that leads to a car park. Go straight across this into Beddington Park, across the footbridge at the tip of Grange Lake. The park is recorded as the location of two manorial estates in the Domesday Book.

Turn right to follow the edge of the lake via a grotto. The formal gardens give way to open parkland, where you follow the track alongside the river to a flint-cobbled bridge that takes you to the opposite bank. Follow the path in the direction of the clock-tower of red-brick Carew Manor, now an adult education centre, but for 500 years was the home of the Carew family, friend of British monarchs through the ages. Turn left to pass in front of the Church of St Mary and the Manor, and then bear left at the timber-framed house to go over a bridge. Turn right, passing cricket pitch and park on the left, to the next bridge of the Wandle. At the end of the row of cottages, go diagonally across the car park and a patch of green. Follow a trickle of river round to the left, then cut right diagonally towards where the top of a dark cedar tree rises above broadleaved woodland. Rejoin the river via an asphalt path where apartment blocks come into view. Over the bridge, go left and head right to the exit gate adorned with concrete spheres. Cross Beddington Lane, go right then turn left over a bridge to follow the right-hand bank of the Wandle.

The path emerges into a small road, where there are some weatherboarded mill cottages that were attached to the nearby Lambert's snuff mill. Go left towards a fine Victorian factory building, turn right in front of it, then take first right into Kingston Gardens. Follow a strip of green between the river and a housing estate on the left. Watercress was grown commercially on the river here until the 1930s. The path turns back into a road again; continue along a patch of green with the river to your right. At the end, cross the river and turn left (signposted Waddon Ponds). Factory buildings lie to the left, and then on your right are a playground and Waddon Ponds, source of the Croydon branch of the Wandle. The pond is the last remaining of several millponds that belonged to the manor of Waddon Court. Walk through the gardens, cross Purley Way and turn left to Waddon Railway Station.

RIBBON OF GREEN: THE BRENT RIVER

Summary: A surprising and delightful ribbon of green countryside winds through the roads, industrial estates and dense suburbia of north-west London. Though it has been notorious in the past for its pollution and still has problems today, the River Brent flows through a band of meadowland rather than the marsh and industrial landscape of the Lea in the east. We see evidence of the river's changing moods, from raging floodwaters to wildlife haven, and a splendid example of Victorian engineering in the Wharncliffe Viaduct at Hanwell.

START:	Perivale Underground Station
FINISH:	Hanwell Railway Station
DISTANCE:	6 miles (10km)
REFRESHMENTS:	Hanwell village or take a picnic!

From the station, turn left and continue to the footbridge that takes you over the A40 road and descends into a brief cul-de-sac. Cross Perivale Lane and almost immediately opposite is a lych gate to the footpath past the tiny church of St Mary the Virgin, which dates back to 1125. Soon after, cross the river and take the first path to the right. At the next junction, take a sharp right down an earthen-gravel path that follows a single curve in the river. This soon rejoins the main path, where you turn right to cut a straight route to the roundabout at Argyle Road. Turn right along the road until you see a path leading on to the playing fields, where the river loops to the north. Cut obliquely across the fields to go behind the swimming pool, just beyond which you will meet the river once more at Ruislip Road East. Turn right under the railway bridge and immediately look for the escape route along a green path squeezed in between river and busy road. Perivale Park, on the opposite side of the river, used to be one of the biggest hay fields in Ealing.

A Ribbon of Green
River and path swing south and you have to cross Ruislip Road East at Greenford Bridge and rejoin the riverside route obliquely opposite. Suddenly, as the traffic noise recedes behind, a ribbon of green countryside emerges, which you can

follow with only minor interruptions all the way to the River Thames at Brentford by linking with *A Flight of Locks* walk (see pages 20–27). Admittedly, if the river is low – and its level varies according to the season and the flow from Welsh Harp (or Brent) Reservoir upstream – its exposed banks will be littered with shreds of plastic and other rubbish. Occasionally, the locals form a working party to clear the river of its litter and now Ealing Council has hired a contractor to do the job full-time. Even at its worst, however, the condition of the river is a vast improvement on how it was at the turn of the century, when it was so polluted with raw effluent from sewage works at Wembley, Hendon and Hanwell that all the fish, and even the water rats, were killed off.

You can see how dramatically the river's flow changes by observing the deposits of shingle, the high, stepped terraces on the banks and the water-scoured vegetation. The Brent's waters are fed by streams coming from high gravel terraces to the north, such as Dollis Brook at Barnet, the Silk Stream in Edgware and the Wealdstone in Harrow. In 1901, serious flooding left the streets of Perivale under water. Stretches of the river were tamed and straightened to reduce downstream flooding. Today, the Brent's flow is controlled by sluice gates on the Welsh Harp Reservoir, which open and close automatically depending on the level of water. The reservoir was created in the 1830s by damming the Brent's upper waters and tributaries. Initially, its job was to provide water for the Grand Union and Regent's canals, flowing along a 4-mile (6.7-km) feeder channel that joins the Paddington Arm of the Grand Union (see pages 14–19, *Hay and Bricks* walk), but today it operates as a flood buffer. Even so, with particularly heavy rainfall the reservoir gets full to bursting point; at one point in 1977 the sluice gates were opened and 1,000 cubic feet (28 cubic metres) of water a second rushed into the already swollen Brent.

Riverside Meadows

After heavy rain, and frequently in winter, the riverside path may be waterlogged to begin with. Farther on, however, stretches of smart new, orange gravel paths have been laid for all-season walking. The broad, flat bankside leads to a wide expanse of meadow that is golden with wild grasses in summer, and splashes of purple from thickets of rosebay willowherb. Footbridges lead across the river – you can take the first or the second – to Brent Valley Golf Course, where you turn left to follow a sand and gravel track bordered by hawthorn until eventually arriving at the tubular metal Bowles Bridge, also known as Boles or Bulls Bridge. Stop awhile to read the information board on local wildlife, which highlights exciting summer visitors, such as spotted flycatchers and reed and sedge warblers, which feast on the

Opposite: *When travelling from Windsor to London, Queen Victoria would ask the royal train to stop on the Wharncliffe Viaduct so that she could look at the view along the Brent Valley at Hanwell. The viaduct was designed by Isambard Kingdom Brunel and built in 1836.*

Perivale
Underground
Station

HORSENDEN LANE SOUTH

DAWLISH AVE.

A40
WESTERN AVENUE

PERIVALE LANE

St Mary
the Virgin

Playing
Fields

ARGYLE ROAD

Perivale Park

GREENFORD RD

RUISLIP ROAD EAST

Swimming Pool

Greenford Bridge

River Brent

N

500m (549 yards)

Brent Valley Golf Course

Bowles Bridge

St Mary's Church

CHURCH RD

MANOR COURT RD

GORDON MANOR

CAMPBELL ROAD
Hanwell Railway Station

ALWYNE RD

Brent
Lodge
Park

Viaduct

YORK AVE

STATION RD

CHURCH RD

Hanwell

Church Path

waterside insects. Just after sunset on a summer's evening you may see pipistrelle bats flying in their high-speed, jerky manner, as a colony has chosen these water meadows as a foraging ground. A ditch nearby is evidence of the river's re-routing, for it marks a former course and is the only place in London where a particular species of willow grows that was once used in basket-making.

Brunel Makes His Mark

Across the bridge, turn right. Here you have a choice either to follow the river as it loops through meadows beneath Hanwell (turning right when you meet the metalled path) or taking a high-level route. For the high-level route bear left uphill towards St Mary's Church, which was designed by Sir George Gilbert Scott (1811–78) and completed in 1841; this stands on the site of the original settlement of Hanwell Village and an earlier 12th-century church. Cross the road obliquely in front of the church to enter Brent Lodge Park, which was converted from three big fields that were cultivated in rotation in medieval times. Walk along the avenue across the park.

The valley ahead is spanned by the imposing arches of a railway viaduct constructed in the 1830s by Isambard Kingdom Brunel (1806–59). At the far end of the park head right, downhill, along a narrow metalled path towards the viaduct. (If you took the alternative riverside route, this is where you end up.) Bear left to go through a wooden gate and beneath a towering arch to rejoin the river. To appreciate the full impact of the viaduct, cross the footbridge immediately ahead and walk along the broad grassy path above the river for a few yards before looking back at the great arches striding across the vale. It is said that when Queen Victoria was travelling by private train to Windsor, she asked for the train to stop on the viaduct so that she could enjoy the view of the Brent Valley. Her viewpoint would have been nearly 70 feet (22m) above the valley floor. The eight arches of the viaduct are supported by a pair of hollow brick piers and span 300 yards (274m), although the viaduct's supporting embankment stretches for a total of 1½ miles (2.5km) at the approaches. This is part of Brunel's 120-mile (200-km) Great Western Railway route from London to Bristol, and was his first major design to be completed.

Retrace your steps back across the footbridge and turn sharp right just before the viaduct up a narrow path into Church Path, left under another viaduct arch, right into Golden Manor and right again into Campbell Road, which leads to Hanwell Railway Station.

OLD RIVERS FOR NEW: BOW BACK RIVERS AND OLYMPIC LEGACY

Summary: What used to be an amorphous muddle of run-down industrial estate and housing between Stratford, Bromley and West Ham has been transformed, initially for the 2012 Olympic Games, but for more permanent uses over the next 50 years, as part of the post-Olympic legacy. The 500-acre (2.4 sq km) core Olympic site is fitted into a triangle of land between waterways that feed into the River Lea. We follow these rivers and canals to uncover their action-packed industrial and social past. The former Olympic site has now been reborn as Queen Elizabeth Park, and we find the best routes around its maze of walkways, discovering less-trodden paths and hidden gems of wild gardens.

START:	Stratford International Rail Station
FINISH:	Stratford International Rail Station
DISTANCE:	5 3/4 miles (9.3 km)
REFRESHMENTS:	Westfield mall, Stratford; View Tube Container Café, on the Greenway; Three Mills (supermarket)

From Stratford International, follow signs for Queen Elizabeth Park, crossing Western Avenue to enter the park at the scoop of Aquatics Centre, which houses two Olympic-sized swimming pools and a diving pool with 12 boards, the highest 10m (30 feet) above the water. Go to the north side of the Centre and turn right to follow the eastern bank of Waterworks River, part of the old Bow Back river system that frames the main site of the London Olympic Games.

Tidal waters and channels that once ebbed and flowed over salt-marsh were tamed and impounded through the ages to provide the network of channels that makes up the Bow Back Rivers. Some stretches of them were closed during the Olympic makeover and have only recently been opened. Their names – Pudding

Opposite: *The legacy of the London Olympic Games transformed industrial waste-land and murky waterways into landscaped parkland and prompted a £1.75 million makeover of the 1930s Carpenter's Road Lock that had the only vertical-rising, double-radial lock gates in the country.*

Homerton

Marshgate Bridge

HOMERTON ROAD

EASTWAY

Hackney Cut

HIGH ST

Mabley Green

KENWORTHY RD

BARNABAS RD

MACINTOSH RD

EAST CROSS ROUTE

EASTWAY

ABERCROMBIE RD

River Lea

HONOUR LEA AVE

OLYMPIC PARK AVE

Homerton
Railway
Station

School

Lee Navigation

Hackney
Wick

WATERDEN RD

INTERNATIONAL WAY

Stratford
International

Hackney Wick
Railway Station

WESTFIELD AVE

Westfield
Mall

CARPENTER'S ROAD

Hertford
Union
Canal

Lee Navigation

City River Lea

Stratford
Marsh

Waterworks River

Aquatics
Centre

LOOP RD

Old Ford
Lock

LOOP RD

Pudding Mill River

Olympic
Stadium

City Mill River

River Lea

WARTON RD

HIGH ST

View Tube

City
Mill
Lock

BLAKER RD

Pudding Mill
Lane DLR
Station

DLR

ABBEY LANE

Bow Back
River

HIGH ST

BISSON ROAD

Three Mills Wall River

Abbey Mills
Pumping
Station

Prescott Channel

BOW RD

BLACKWALL TUNNEL NORTHERN APPROACH A12

PENNOCK RD

House
Mill

Three
Mills
Green

THREE MILL LN

subway

Superstore

Clock Mill

IMPERIAL ST

Bow Creek

TV &
Film
Studios

N

500m (549 yards)

Bromley-By-Bow
Underground Station

Mill River, City Mill River, Waterworks River – indicate their hard-working heritage. Once they were busy with barge traffic carrying coal, raw materials and goods to and fro from the industries that developed along their banks in the 19th century. Today's traffic is more likely to be made up of leisure boat trips, refuse barges, and the occasional dredger to clear tidal silt. Now the rivers are constant companions in the post-Olympic, 560-acre Queen Elizabeth Park.

The Waterworks River that you are walking beside was named for a mid-18th-century water company that created an artificial channel from the original tidal tributary of the River Lea in order to feed a reservoir in Stratford. The bed of the waterway is lined with concrete slabs, but its banks are now a glorious riot of flowers from spring to early autumn, a legacy of the Olympic Games. Soil — 1.4 million tons of it — was lifted from the Olympic building site, then washed and purified before being relaid in the new landscape. Planting followed themes: around the main stadium, yellow flowers predominate for the 'Olympic Gold Meadows'; elsewhere northern-European meadows, prairie and woodland of temperate America, and the bush vegetation of Australasia and South Africa are evoked.

Reconstituted Wetlands

Reach Carpenters Lock, which was originally built in the 1930s to stem flooding in the Lower Lea Valley. Today, the gleaming metal curves of the footbridges that span the confluence of old River Lea and Bow Back rivers, and the still waterways below give two-way reflections. The route continues north, over Carpenters Road and across Waterden Road, along the broad boulevard of London Way. Turn right at the first footbridge over the River Lea, then go down the first steps right. At the foot of the steps, turn left, go straight ahead at the crossing, and head towards the graveled entrance of 'Waterglades'. Now take the first path to the right, leading back into the wetlands to circuit the southern edge of the most striking pond of all, which is bordered by purple loosestrife and floating with golden water lilies in high summer. Water from roofs of the apartment blocks overlooking the ponds – the former Olympic Village – is cleaned and treated in these wetlands and returned to flush toilets and water landscaped areas on the estate. Look out for ecology installations – there are 150 of them, including bird and bat boxes and invertebrate and insect logs.

Follow the path round to the right, then continue straight ahead until you see steps ahead, but turn left before them. Pass the steps you came down from the bridge, and follow the path round to the left, cross a footbridge, then turn right to go between artistically arranged sections of red public telephone box, down to the river.

This lesser populated, newly landscaped east bank of the Lea is a lovely walk lined with reeds, grasses and marsh flowers. Farther on, above right, on the former site of the largest used-refrigerator dump in Europe, the roller-coaster structure of the Velodrome was built for the Olympics, but you won't be able to see it until you look back from the opposite bank of the river.

Pass beneath a couple of heavy-duty iron girder bridges, and three bridge-spans later, bear right where you see a path leading up to a busy road. Turn left along the road, over the river, then go sharp left at 5-bar wooden gate, signed Queen Elizabeth Park, to drop to the west bank. Pass under the iron girder bridges again, then bear right up to the pedestrian boulevard of London Way. As one of the Park's main thoroughfares, this boulevard has a completely different 'vibe' to the east bank. To the right is the former press and broadcasting centre, which was built with a deliberate lack of windows to allow for around-the-clock broadcasting during the Olympics and kitted out for 20,000 members of the world press. It is being reborn as a high-tech commercial centre. In contrast, the boulevard is lined on the left with native trees, such as mountain ash, apple and cherry.

Yellow flag iris

You retrace the outward route for a brief section over Waterden Road to Mandeville Place. The Stadium is straight ahead, a shadow of its Olympic self. For the Games, a concrete framework for the 80,000-seat stadium was constructed and then the roof lifted into place. Now, the top layers have been removed to leave a permanent 25,000-seat structure. Short of the stadium, just beyond and below the first footbridge leading off the south corner of Mandeville Place, look left for broad wooden steps, which lead down, away from the more populated upper routes, to the confluence of the rivers at Carpenters Lock. Turn right beneath the gleaming arches and cross a footbridge through a charming secret garden with simple but striking sculptures, and a lily pond. The path leads through a natural willow bower back up to the main path, where you turn left.

The Green Line of the Sewer

This area is in a state of flux due to continuing development and the Crossrail underground network. At the time of writing, a diversion cuts down to the right from the Stadium to join the Lee Navigation channel. Turn left here, to pass Old Ford Lock (you follow this section in the opposite direction on the *Short Cuts to Limehouse* walk, p. 28) and keep heading southwards to cross the River Lea again, via a footbridge, to its east bank. Pass under giant pipes that mark the course of the Greenway, the flattering name for the course of the Northern

Outfall Sewer, a mighty pipe that 'intercepted' waste from throughout north and west London and carried it to be discharged into the Thames east of the City. At first, the waste was untreated as it flowed into the Thames; the pipes still carry sewage to this day, but happily it is now treated at a plant in Beckton to the southeast. The network of interceptor sewage pipes was devised by metropolitan engineer Sir Joseph Bazalguette (1819–91) and was the first effective step towards solving London's dreadful problems of flooding cesspits, foul-smelling rivers running with raw sewage and frequent outbreaks of cholera.

To visit the acid-green container complex of View Tube café and information centre, you can simply continue straight ahead along the Greenway instead of taking the diversion down to the Lee Navigation at the Works near the Olympic Stadium. However, for the time being at least, it is a dead-end on our waterway route, which, to rejoin, you must retrace your steps to the cut down to the Lee.

The Lee soon joins the original River Lea, and you continue until a zig-zagging footbridge and take it to cross to the opposite bank and then turn left. Look over the water to ongoing development with a red-brick chimney leftover from a bygone time. A little farther on, you will find a weir at the entrance to the Three Mills Wall River. Just beyond this, go up the cobbled rise that leads up to Three Mills Lane. Turn left to Three Mills Island, an enclave of courtyards running between House Mill (left) and Clock Mill (right). These are all that survive of the many mills that once utilized the tidal power of the Bow Back Rivers.

A Whiff of Gin

If you go to the landscaped area south of the Mill complex, you can look down into the mud-thick river, smell the salty air and see the millstream route beneath the buildings. At low tide, there is little but a narrow ribbon of murky water worming its way through slopes of darkly gleaming mud. It was the power of the receding tide that was harnessed by these mills when they were in operation. The incoming tidal flow was channelled into the millrace and the floodgates beyond were lowered to trap it; then, when the tide turned, the gates were raised and the outflow turned the waterwheels.

You can still see much of the internal mill machinery, including the huge waterwheels and six pairs of millstones, inside House Mill on the left of the cobbled courtyard. In its day, House Mill was one of the most powerful tidal mills in England. It last worked in 1941 as a distillery but has now been restored as a listed industrial site. Corn was ground here and at many other sites locally – eight are recorded in the 1086 Domesday Book – helping the nearby village of Stratforde-atte-Bowe (modern Bow) to build up a reputation as the centre for providing London's bread. Three Mills was originally part of an abbey that was destroyed during Henry VIII's dissolution of the monasteries in the 1530s. The two surviving mills became privately owned, and one was turned over to grinding gunpowder in 1588. In the 18th century came the establishment of a distillery business combined with a piggery that supplied the British Navy with pork. The tide-powered millstones ground grain for gin over a period of 165 years from the 18th century. The alcohol connection continued into the 20th century: Clock Mill, with its on-site oast house for drying grain, was, until recent decades, the headquarters of the wine and spirit arm of Bass Brewers. The present building dates from 1817.

Good Intentions
With House Mill on your left and Clock Mill to the right, head for the blue painted metal gates of the film studios, home of the reality TV show *Big Brother*. Peter Bazalguette, whose company produces the programme, is the great-great grandson of Joseph Bazalguette, the Victorian engineer who routed London sewage outlets through this area.

Turn left up the wide asphalt path to a junction marked by a big London plane tree. Go straight across, briefly to the path bordering the left of Three Mills Green, to see a sculpture of clasped hands, which commemorates people who died 'in the course of their work' on the waterways in 1901. Victims included a Customs and Excise officer who was 'overcome by foul air' and 'those who descended to save him suffered the same death'.

Return to the plane tree junction, and turn left to go along the road along the south side of the Green. Just short of the main entrance to the film studios, go through a pedestrian gate in the black park railings, and see Three Mills Lock ahead. The upgraded lock was intended to 'create a green gateway for barges entering the Olympic Park, helping to remove up to 1,000 lorry journeys a week from local roads', thus cutting fuel usage and pollution by around a third and a sixth, respectively, and improving local air quality by cutting 4,000 tonnes of carbon dioxide. Unfortunately, it was reported that vessels ran aground on the inland side of the lock because there wasn't enough water. The project allegedly doubled its initial budget, coincided with an economic crisis and had to compete against falling road haulage rates, so invalidating the original aims.

The lock spans the Prescott Channel, which was cut in the 1930s to channel floodwaters – the water coming down from Bedfordshire often spilled over the low-lying levels as the Lea approached the Thames. Today, the wind blows in from the estuary, downstream from the lock, mingling intense odours of saltwater, tidal mud and traffic fumes. In the bad old days, there was additional pollution from chemical factories that contaminated air, ground and water. Over recent decades, fish such as pike, perch and eel returned to the waterways — that is, until the upheaval of the Olympic Park construction. However, the Olympic Delivery Authority relocated fish to the River Lea, and 2,000 newts and hundreds of toads to specially constructed ponds.

Improvements on the Bad Old Days

From the lock you can see a grey, slate-roofed building with a neo-Gothic Victorian red-and-green central tower. This is the 'Cathedral of Sewage', or more correctly, Abbey Mills Pumping Station, built as the operating centre of an innovatory Victorian sewage system. It is now redundant, replaced by the large grey building to its right.

With Three Mills Lock behind you, bear right across the Green over a hill with a natural play park, across a footbridge, then go diagonally left to follow a path bordering Three Mills Wall River. In the early 19th century, this stretch must have been pleasant, lined with the osier beds that produced the raw materials for basketmaking. But we are approaching the area that became known as 'Stinky Stratford', when factories producing printing inks, glue and asphalt, banned from operating in London under an 1844 Pollution Act, moved to the Lea Valley. Instead of the Thames, it was the Bow Back Rivers that took the uncontrolled, untreated flow of industrial effluent. Now, thanks to the Olympic Park and its long-term legacy, Stratford is, they say, the focus of the largest urban redevelopment in Europe. The legacy plans take the development and maintenance of the area beyond the games and 50 years into the future.

Reach the main road – Stratford High Street – cross and turn right. Somewhere among the continuing redevelopment here flows the Bow Back River, former dump for uncontrolled, untreated industrial effluent, and a meeting with the Greenway path. When the path is reopened, it will provide direct access back into the Queen Elizabeth Park and the return to Stratford International. Until then, you have to continue to the left, turn down Warton Road and continue under the railway bridge to the Park entrance on the left at the roundabout. Go over the railway up to the main path and turn right, then right again at the main avenue just before the Aquatic Centre and follow signs to the Stratford International Station.

THE LEA'S MARSHY ORIGINS: LEA RIVER LOOP AND HACKNEY

Summary: Discover the Old River Lea and how humans have tamed it in the service of transport and industry and in order to control the floods that have plagued the river's lower levels. As a London waterway system, the Lea is second in importance only to the Thames and has provided a key transport and communications route, a focus for waterside industries, a source of rich meadows for cultivation and grazing and a vital water supply for the city and its suburbs. It is also an important leisure facility for Londoners. Make sure you do this walk at a weekend to take advantage of the Middlesex Filter Beds Nature Reserve, an evocative blend of industrial ruins reclaimed by wildlife.

START AND FINISH:	Homerton Railway Station
DISTANCE:	6 miles (10km)
REFRESHMENTS:	Pubs at Lea Bridge; café at Springfield Marina

From Homerton Station, head north to the main Homerton Road and turn right. Soon you pass Mabley Green, right, its flat expanse broken by a solitary lump of Cornish granite, which is used as a climbing boulder. Cross the waterway – Hackney Cut – at Marshgate Bridge, turn right at an arrangement of rocks set into the pavement, into Wick Wood, then turn right again to follow the canal north. Hackney Cut is a 2-mile (3.2km) stretch of the Lee Navigation (the artificially channelled course of the old River Lea) between the weir at Middlesex Filter Beds to the north and Old Ford Lock to the south. It was excavated in 1768 to bypass a meander in the old River Lea and facilitate navigation. As the name 'Marshgate' suggests, we are at the edge of Hackney Marsh.

Opposite: *Belted Galloways from south-west Scotland are known for their good nature, hardiness and longevity. They have been introduced to the Lea's managed marshlands to maintain the ecosystem that has been established there.*

To add the word 'marsh' is tautological, for the word Hackney comes from *haca's eoth*, meaning 'well-watered land or marsh'. The marsh became a public open space in 1894. For centuries it had been 'lammas land', that is, it could be cultivated by those who had a share in it only between 6 April and 12 August, while for the rest of the year it was common land for grazing. Today, much of the marshland has been largely filled in and transformed into playing fields fringed by trees. The original marshland has been drained systematically since medieval times, and after the Second World War much of Main Marsh – the playing fields fringed with trees on your right – was filled in with the rubble of buildings destroyed by bombs, which raised the level of the land. Wick Wood just on the other side of Marshgate Bridge, received no infill, and so is lower-lying, but trees, such as the native species planted during the 1990s, take more quickly as their roots didn't have to push through rubble.

Green and Pleasant

The route is generally green and pleasant now, as this stretch appears to be better maintained than in the past. There may be patches of duckweed floating on the sluggish water in high summer, which, if it builds up, reduces oxygen, but the invasive Japanese knotweed that plagued it for years has been cleared, and there is less floating rubbish. There are many more residential narrow-boats too, a cheaper alternative to bricks and mortar for first-time home buyers.

Pass beneath a lime-green, caged-in footbridge. Beyond it, over to the left, is a big, red-brick warehouse, which was reborn as a refuse disposal depot. Another bridge, enclosed this time in grey corrugated iron, is followed by an open space, whose name of South Mill Fields recalls the thriving water-powered industry here during the 18th century. To your right, a curving wall echoes the course of the towpath. Beyond it are the Middlesex Filter Beds, now a nature reserve and a magical retreat where the old channels, beds and paths of a defunct water-treatment works lie among the luxuriant natural vegetation of the Lea's marshland. The filter beds were built in a bid to purify the River Lea's water supply following the 1849 cholera epidemic that claimed the lives of 14,000 East Londoners. The evocative industrial memorabilia includes rails, a sand trolley, sluice gates, the central filtering culvert and dried-up channels and tanks. Water treatment ceased in 1969 and now this haven attracts more than 60 species of birds, including some that stop here for a rest on their migration routes, while crevices in the brick and concrete provide cosy hibernation spots for amphibians.

From the main entrance, which is on the right just before the bridge over the Navigation, follow the nature reserve path to the left and then go right, to where the Old River Lea is flowing free of the Navigation. The river's waters are

High Bridge

Coppermill Bridge

SPRING HILL

Horse Shoe Bridge

Springfield Marina

Walthamstow Marshes

Lea Valley Riding Centre

N

500m (549 yards)

Sewer pipe

Lee Valley Ice Centre

North Mill Fields

LEA BRIDGE ROAD

The Waterworks Nature Reserve

Lea Bridge Weir

Pub

Pub

Footbridge

WATERWORKS LANE

South Mill Fields

Middlesex Filter Beds Nature Reserve

Lea Bridge

River Lea

Hackney Marsh

Hackney Marshes Centre

Marshgate Bridge

HOMERTON ROAD

Homerton

BARNABAS RD

HIGH ST

KENWORTHY RD

Mabley Green

Hackney Cut

MACKINTOSH RD

Homerton Railway Station

still governed by sluices, but here it begins to look like a real river. You can see nothing of them now, but back in the 18th century there were busy mills on this site. The brisk, channelled flow fed waterwheels to power the boring of tree trunks to make the precursors of iron water pipes. A second mill ground grain and the energy from a third powered machinery to sharpen pins and needles (the needles were then shipped to Worcestershire to have eyes inserted). The locks and sluices that controlled the water level and flow were good news for the milling business, but put the millers at odds with the boatmen who wanted clear, direct waterways to and from London; the Hackney Cut was dug between here and Old Ford to bypass the mills and bring a halt to the arguing.

Divergence and Convergence
After circuiting the nature reserve, return to the gate you entered by and turn right back on to the towpath. Cross the steep footbridge, with its treads or 'scorchers' for horses, on to the left bank and turn right along the towpath over another footbridge. Look across the water to the right to a weir: beneath unusual overhead 'guillotine'-style lock gates, the Old River Lea breaks away from the Navigation.

There are pub stops here on the waterside and up on the road. Continue along the towpath past Millfields Recreation ground, and follow the united waters of the river and the Navigation in a broad sweep to the right. Shortly, you cross the river over another ridged footbridge, and take a high gravel path bordering Walthamstow Marshes. Continue under the railway bridge until you reach the next bridge (Horse Shoe Bridge).

Pass Springfield Park left and the marina left, then cross the river again over High Bridge to skirt Springfield Marina. Follow the path leading to the left of the marina. Continue straight ahead at an open gravel area with an iron gateway and a map of the Walthamstow Marshes. Just before the railway embankment bisects the way ahead, turn right onto the reclaimed marshes. Now, just follow the well-trodden paths across the open grassland in a generally diagonal direction to where the railway bridge crosses the river.

The marshes are rich in waterside plants, including yellow flag iris and creamy meadowsweet, followed by purple loosestrife and Michaelmas daisies in late summer. When the water table is high, you can get an impression of the waterlogged channels, their courses marked by reeds and sedges, which are traces of meltwater courses formed at the end of the last ice age.

Over Marsh and Meadow
Go under the railway bridge and turn immediately left along a boardwalk over the marshes. At the end of the boardwalk, continue straight ahead over grazing

meadows, where you may see old English Longhorns and Belted Galloway cattle. The animals have been reintroduced after a 100-year absence and hay is cut to maintain the distinctive ecosystem that has evolved here from a combination of wild and managed land. The first major impact on the water level came in AD 896, when King Alfred the Great ordered both damming and draining of the Lea Levels at various points to alter the course of the upstream river and make it too shallow to be navigated by the Danish invaders. This enterprise, plus the cutting of additional drainage channels over the centuries, turned the marsh into meadowland. From the Middle Ages, this area was lammas land, until common grazing ceased around a century ago.

Across the meadow, climb to a metalled path that follows the course of an aqueduct until the path splits at a left turn to the Lea Valley Riding Centre; go straight on, under a fat sewer pipe and a road bridge. You soon pass, left, on the opposite side of the river from the Middlesex Filter Beds, another nature reserve, this one on the site of a waterworks. Follow the path left through an iron gate and cross a red-winged footbridge over the river, to playing fields. Turn left along the asphalt path; farther along you can cut left to a lower, wooded trail that hugs the broad, clear, winding course of the old river. The riverside path rejoins the metalled road eventually, and the sound of traffic begins to intrude upon the peace. After passing a footbridge on the left, look for the entrance to a car park and Hackney Marsh Centre on the right, and turn into it. Go immediately right to the recreation ground, and cross it diagonally left towards the high rise flats at Marshgate Bridge, then turn right at Homerton Road, past Mabley Green and back to the station.

Purple loosestrife

RURAL BROOKS: DOLLIS, FOLLY AND MUTTON

Summary: This is a nature ramble of a walk, offering rich tree-spotting opportunities. As the vale roller-coasters gently through unseen surrounding suburbs, you get an idea of how the landscape of the London basin was formed millions of years ago. If the weather forecast is good, take a picnic, for there are plenty of spots to stop at and no riverside cafés. Although the route threads its way through suburbs such as Totteridge and Hampstead Garden Suburb, these are hidden beyond the green vale of the walk. It is an all-weather route, as the path is mostly metalled. There are various points at which you can stop and start the walk.

START:	High Barnet Underground Station
FINISH:	East Finchley Underground Station (or various undergrounds en route)
DISTANCE:	6 or 9 miles (10 or 15km)
REFRESHMENTS:	shops and pubs on main roads that cross the route at High Barnet, Totteridge & Whetstone, East Finchley

In the Wake of the Sea

The Dollis and Mutton brooks rise on remnants of the clay and gravel ridges that are a feature of the London Basin landscape. Fifty million years ago, a warm tropical sea covered all of southern England and, as it retreated, the clays that had settled on its floor were left behind. There was a great river, too, in the broad, shallow vale, and over the next million years its sluggish waters, heavy with sand and mud carried from upstream waters, flooded the plain. Gradually the climate changed, the land rose and the river shrank, leaving layers of sand and gravel in its wake. Over further aeons of geological time, later watercourses scoured the layers of clay and sand, remnants of which can be seen in the high spots of what are now London suburbs, such as Highgate (where Mutton Brook rises), Totteridge (to the north of which lies the Dollis watershed), Hampstead Heath and, south of the present course of the Thames, Shooter's Hill, near Blackheath.

We start on one of these ridges – at High Barnet – and look down over suburbia to the south and east. From the underground station turn left and walk

Dogwood

through the car park and up the slip road. Cross the main road at the top and turn left. Turn right at end of the slip-road, and right again into Fairfield Way. Continue straight ahead into Grasvenor Avenue until you see the entrance to Underhill playing fields on the right. Take this path and, at the first junction, where you turn left, you can see the course of Dollis Brook in a waving course from the west as a band of dark green backed by tall poplars. Beyond rises the suburb of Totteridge, protected common land for centuries and an island of green in suburbia.

Visions of an Ancient Forest

When you reach the brook take the left turn, as the Dollis abruptly changes its course to flow southwards. Look back towards High Barnet and imagine the land covered in the oak woodland of the pre-glacial Great Middlesex Forest. The name Barnet means a clearing burnt in the woods, harking back to the Saxons' slash-and-burn techniques as they destroyed vast tracts of Britain's ancient forests. As the metalled path wends its way through stretches of well-maintained grass, or threads through wooded glades, the mood is more or less set for the entire walk. The dark shades of oak, elder, alder and dogwood are set off by the silvered greys and greens of willow and poplar. The Dollis, however, is out of sight for much of the way, enshrouded by a thick cover of nettles and shrubs, though you catch a glimpse of the occasional meander. In summer the flow is too slow and shallow to provide clear waters.

Your route straight ahead is clear to the first road crossing of Totteridge Lane. A possible stop/start point at Totteridge and Whetstone Underground Station is a short way to the left. Turn right and cross the road opposite the handful of shops to follow the opposite side of the brook. The heart of Totteridge – an extraordinary enclave of common land and charming detached houses, more like a Buckinghamshire village than a London suburb – is way up the hill to your right. It is possible to make a detour (marked on the map with broken lines) via the common, a 'village' pond and Folly Brook, a trickle of

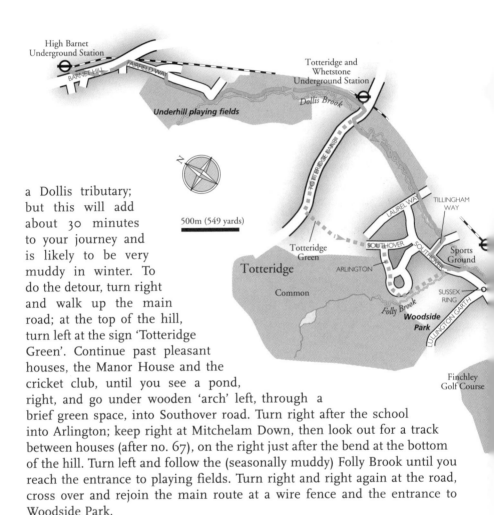

a Dollis tributary;
but this will add
about 30 minutes
to your journey and
is likely to be very
muddy in winter. To
do the detour, turn right
and walk up the main
road; at the top of the hill,
turn left at the sign 'Totteridge
Green'. Continue past pleasant
houses, the Manor House and the
cricket club, until you see a pond,
right, and go under wooden 'arch' left, through a
brief green space, into Southover road. Turn right after the school
into Arlington; keep right at Mitchelam Down, then look out for a track
between houses (after no. 67), on the right just after the bend at the bottom
of the hill. Turn left and follow the (seasonally muddy) Folly Brook until you
reach the entrance to playing fields. Turn right and right again at the road,
cross over and rejoin the main route at a wire fence and the entrance to
Woodside Park.

Dollis Meets Folly

The direct route, excluding the Totteridge diversion above, crosses Totteridge
Lane and then meanders with the Dollis along a delightful broad and gently
rolling valley. A metal gate announces the next road crossing – Laurel Way –
and then a white-barred gate into Riverside Walk and a pleasant park and
playground area. At the end of this, turn right into Tillingham Way, continue
to the junction with the broad Southover, and turn left. (Alternatively, there's
another stop/start point left along Tillingham Way, then right and left to
Woodside Park Underground Station.) Pass the football ground on your left

and, at a high wire fence, turn left into Woodside Park, the point at which the Folly and Dollis meet.

Keep the stream to left as the path meanders through parks. After crossing Fursby Avenue (where you can turn left towards West Finchley Underground Station), pass between smart and productive allotments before the trees close in on the path as it follows the course of the Dollis, now set between steep banks carved by floodwaters. Follow the stream over a hump-backed footbridge, then take a right at the junction. Up right are glimpses of Finchley Golf Course. Turn left to cross another bridge; the Dollis and a pond behind it are now on your right. Where the path forks, go right and cross the next bridge (a left fork here

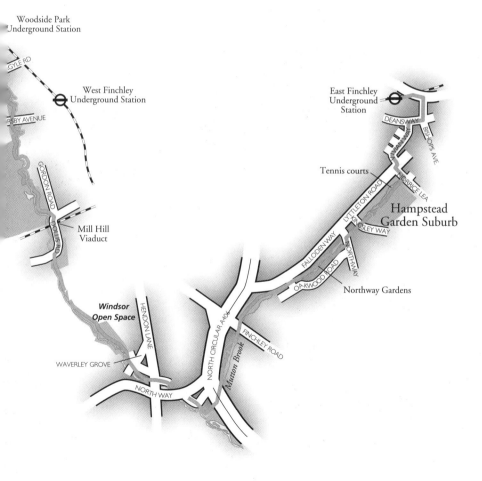

Woodside Park Underground Station

GYLE RD

West Finchley Underground Station

East Finchley Underground Station

RSBY AVENUE

DEANSWAY

BISHOPS AVE

Tennis courts

NOBRICE LEA

GORDON ROAD

Hampstead Garden Suburb

LYTTLETON ROAD

Mill Hill Viaduct

DOLLIS RD

KINGSLEY WAY

FALLODEN WAY

NORTHWAY

OAKWOOD ROAD

Northway Gardens

Windsor Open Space

HENDON LANE

WAVERLEY GROVE

NORTH CIRCULAR A406

FINCHLEY ROAD

Mutton Brook

NORTH WAY

would take you to Gordon Road). The pond is still on your right – and turn immediately left. Wind through the trees until you meet Dollis Road. Turn right and immediately before you is Mill Hill Viaduct.

A Victorian Marvel

Sadly, our only view of the viaduct is from the road, but look up left and right for a wonderful perspective of its 13 arches. The viaduct was built in 1867 to carry a section of the London North Eastern Railway, which terminated at Liverpool Street, but now carries the underground's Northern Line. Cross the road before the blind bend, and, just after crossing the Dollis, turn left and immediately left again to cross the river, then right to rejoin the riverside path. Continue through to a broad basin of more parkland, which is known as Windsor Open Space. Across Waverley Grove there are healthy clumps of comfrey. The path dips beneath Hendon Lane, through a slightly soiled but very short underpass, and suddenly the Dollis is almost river-like as it passes over a big concrete-stepped weir. Proceed under North Way, keep right at a junction of paths, then, at a triangle of green play park, turn left. This clear junction of streams, where the Mutton joins the Dollis from the east, is where Dollis Brook is no more: it becomes the Brent River and heads south, then west, to the Welsh Harp (Brent) Reservoir.

We, however, are following Mutton Brook to the east, going beneath a white bridge carrying the North Circular Road. The pretty stretch that follows is like a microcosm of rural southern England – apart from the roar of traffic from the arterial roads that border it and which we keep on encountering. Finchley Road is the first. Cross over and rejoin the path directly opposite. For the next stretch, you can follow either side of the stream. The left bank is more open. If you take the woodland way over the footbridge, make sure that at the end of it, after a grassy strip and a right turn to a road, you cross left over a footbridge and then bear right up to Falloden Way. Walk along this busy road, past a tiny patch of wildlife and gardens on the right, past the entrance to Oakwood Road, across the road bridge over the brook, then turn right to rejoin the stream on its left bank.

Through Park and Garden

From now on, the route is through more formal municipal parks. Simply follow the course of the brook through Northway Gardens, across Northway and then

Opposite: *Compared to the mighty docks, the River Thames and the hard-working suburban rivers, the Mutton Brook is tiny and purely decorative as it flows through the parkland bordering Hampstead Garden Suburb.*

Kingsley Way, into Lyttleton Playing Fields. You can take any of the eastward routes through the park, but if you keep left, you can see apartment blocks whose style reflects the spirit of Hampstead Garden Suburb, which borders the park to the south. The suburb was created from 1907 onwards, when the underground reached Golder's Green, and was the inspiration of Dame Henrietta Barnett, who envisaged a perfectly balanced community with a range of traditional English building styles and sizes, from craftsmen's cottages to Georgian-style mansions.

Pass to the right-hand side of the tennis courts at the far end of the park. Exit the park into Norrice Lea, and turn left. Cross the main Lyttleton Road and go obliquely right up Vivian Way, which you follow all the way round to its junction with Deansway. Turn right and then left along Bishops Avenue and finally left at the junction to East Finchley Underground Station.

BRIDGING THE THAMES: WESTMINSTER– SOUTHWARK RETURN

Summary: There was a time when one of the most efficient ways of crossing the Thames at anywhere but London Bridge was to 'take the water' and hail a passing wherry or, if you had goods to transport, a lighter. We go on foot to find out more about watermen and lightermen and pass many of the bridges that they feared would make their ferry services redundant. We skim the culture-packed South Bank, pausing only to delve more deeply into buildings that have been influenced by or have some connection with the river.

START AND FINISH:	Westminster Underground Station
DISTANCE:	4 miles (6.7km)
REFRESHMENTS:	Royal Festival Hall; Gabriel's Wharf; Victoria Embankment Gardens.

Monuments of Church and State

From the Bridge Street exit of Westminster Underground Station, in the shadow of the Clock Tower – better known as Big Ben for its 16-ton bell – turn right and cross the road at the statue of Winston Churchill into Parliament Square. Walk the length of the Houses of Parliament on your left. Across the road you can see St Margaret's Westminster, the late medieval church of the House of Commons and the burial place of Elizabethan adventurer and explorer Sir Walter Raleigh (c.1552–1618).

The Houses of Parliament are built on the site of William the Conqueror's Palace of Westminster, but most of the current buildings are the 19th-century Gothic Revival confection of architects Charles Barry (1795–1860) and Augustus Pugin (1812–52), who went to town on the decorative features. Access to the river frontage here, at Lambeth Reach, is confined to politicians and friends, who sip summer sundowners on the terraces beneath striped awnings – red for Lords, green for Commons. In 1605 the Reach was the point at which Guy Fawkes (1570–1606) and his fellow Catholic conspirators in the Gunpowder Plot crossed the river with the aim of blowing up king and Parliament during that year's State opening.

After you pass the 'Sovereign's Entrance' of Victoria Tower, turn left to walk through Victoria Tower Gardens, where there is a statue of the suffragette Emmeline Pankhurst (1858–1928). Further on you pass a Gothic-style fountain memorial to Thomas Buxton, a leading figure in the abolition of the trade in African slaves. Go up the steps at the end of the gardens and turn left over Lambeth Bridge. Until the 19th century, the only river crossing here was by a ferry that was geared to carrying coach and horses as well as foot passengers, and gave its name to Horseferry Road, the north-bank approach to the river. The present 1932 structure replaced an earlier rusting and unsafe suspension bridge and is painted red, the livery of the House of Lords, while Westminster Bridge downstream is Commons green. At the pineapple-topped obelisks that mark each end of Lambeth Bridge, turn left on to the Albert Embankment, which, together with Victoria and Chelsea Embankments on the north side of the river, was masterminded by Sir Joseph Bazalguette, Chief Engineer to the Metropolitan Board of Works. Not only did Sir Joseph dramatically transform the appearance of the riverside, confining the Thames to a narrower, safer and more orderly course, but he also incorporated road, underground and sewage services.

Immediately on your right, across the road, is the red-brick Lambeth Palace, the London seat of the Archbishop of Canterbury. In times past, at high tide, the river reached its entrance. Adjacent to the Archbishop's Palace is the Tradescant Museum of Garden History, formerly St Mary's Church. The museum is named after the 17th-century explorer-botanists John Tradescant the elder (d. 1637) and his son, who was also called John (1608–62), both of whom are buried in the grounds. The elder Tradescant travelled to Europe and Russia and introduced many new plants to Britain, including summer-flowering jasmine and the Persian lilac. His son made several trips to America, bringing back such plants as *Aquilegia Canadensis, Rudbeckia laciniata* and many trees and shrubs. The tomb of Admiral William Bligh (1754–1817), former captain of HMS *Bounty*, is also here.

Doing the Lambeth Walk

Some say that the name Lambeth suggests that this was a landing place for sheep, others that the 'beth' relates, rather appropriately, to the archbishop, as it comes from the Hebrew word meaning 'a sacred place'. In the 17th and 18th centuries, what is now the flagstoned Lambeth Walk was a stretch of shore broken by wooden wharves and overlooked by tumbledown houses, timber and boat yards, with mills and potteries behind. Continue to Westminster Bridge, which you come to next. To see the great lion that guards the bridge you must go up the steps and cross the road. The lion was sculpted from coade stone made at a local factory in 1837 to Ms Eleanor Coade's secret recipe, which has since been lost. If you don't want to see the lion, keep straight along the path under the bridge.

The Westminster Bridge of 1750 became London's second bridging point after London Bridge. Until this time, there was only a wooden bridge at Putney until Kingston. The construction of the original Westminster Bridge was opposed by City bankers and merchants, who were afraid it would take business away from their part of town. The bridge was also sabotaged by watermen who operated the cross-river ferries and plagued by financial problems, bad weather and even a small earthquake. Not surprisingly, perhaps, the bridge took 10 years to build. Over the next 100 years, though, its foundations were weakened by river currents and the original bridge was replaced by the present-day cast-iron one in 1862. Look on the bridge wall right to see a plaque engraved with part of William Wordsworth's poem *On Westminster Bridge*.

Jasmine

There is no need for route instructions now; you just continue along the Queen's Walk (marking Elizabeth II's Silver Jubilee in 1977), passing the grey mass of the former County Hall buildings, which were designed by Ralph Knott between 1908 and 1922, and are now home to fast-food restaurants, the Film Museum, the London Aquarium and booking offices for the London Eye. Then comes the giant ferris wheel itself. Jubilee Gardens lies beyond, with the 1963 Shell Centre behind. The striking Hungerford footbridges, which run on either side of the iron rail bridge, were completed in 2001. They are the second suspension footbridges to be constructed at this point. The first footbridge, whose piers still support the railway bridge, was designed by Isambard Kingdom Brunel, whose father Marc produced the rather less savoury pedestrian crossing of the Thames Tunnel (see pages 100–10, *Wharves and Warehouses* walk).

The City's Cultural Hub

Enjoy downstream views of the river as you follow the curve beneath Waterloo Bridge, passing the 1951 Royal Festival Hall, which was built for the Festival of Britain, Queen Elizabeth Hall, the National Film Theatre and, after the bridge, the National Theatre, which was built amid much controversy in the 1970s. The first Waterloo Bridge, which opened in 1816, was originally called Strand Bridge, but was renamed on the second anniversary of the Duke of Wellington's famous victory over the French. Once again, the scouring force of the river's tides and currents undermined the foundations and the bridge was closed in the 1920s. A new bridge was begun in 1937, but the outbreak of the Second World War delayed work, and the concrete piers were bomb-damaged. Nevertheless, the bridge opened in 1945 and, with its 1,250-foot (380-m) span, it is the longest of London's bridges.

Gabriel's Wharf, with its *trompe-l'oeil* paintings, cafés and craft shops, is an attractive refreshment stop. Continue, passing the Art Deco Oxo Tower on your right (you can take a lift to a viewing gallery on the top floor), passing the river frontage of Sea Container House to Blackfriars Bridge.

Just before the bridge is the Doggett's pub, interesting more for its name than its appearance. Thomas Doggett was an Irish actor and comedian who was so inspired by the Thames watermen and their practice of racing each other from one pick-up point to another, that in 1715 he founded an annual sculling race that is still held to this day. The course, running from London Bridge to Chelsea, is over 4 miles (6.7km) long, and is 'a test of watermenship and endurance, which... are the qualities required of a man who is going to get his living... as a waterman or lighterman'. The winner is awarded, as in times past, with a silver arm badge, scarlet coat and breeches – a 'Livery and Buttons and Appurtenances to it' – based on the uniform of an 18th-century waterman. The Company of Watermen and Lightermen was established in 1555 to introduce some control over the service that was so essential to the movement of goods and people.

Continue beneath Blackfriars Bridge, with its archive lithographs of bridge designs reproduced on the tiles. The polished granite piers of the road bridge, with their Corinthian-style heads, are of Joseph Cubitt's design. The bridge was built in the 1860s and was widened c.1910. Still standing in the river are chunky piers: all that remain of the original rail bridge. The end columns, topped by the cast-iron insignia of the London Chatham and Dover Railway Company, which was responsible for the original 1864 rail crossing, are fine examples of the ornate painted ironwork so beloved of the Victorians.

The Rebirth of Bankside

Beyond Blackfriars Bridge, which now carries 'the first new station on the South Bank for 120 years', you are in the part of the South Bank, which during the 16th and 17th centuries, was the place to be for entertainment such as bear-baiting, cavorting with 'working girls' in the stews (saunas) and, of course, drama (at the Globe Theatre). Now the main focus of attraction is the monumental Tate Modern. The art gallery is housed in the former Bankside Power Station, which was designed by Sir Giles Gilbert Scott (1880–1960), completed in 1952 and closed 30 years later. The suspended walkway of the Millennium Bridge laid claim to being the first footbridge across the London Thames for 100 years, but it had to close soon after its opening because it was unstable; happily, it is now reinforced and in use. Shortly after the footbridge, look right to a row of 17th-century houses at Cardinal's Wharf, purportedly named after Cardinal Wolsey (c.1474–1530), Lord Chancellor to King Henry VIII. It was in one of these houses that the architect Christopher Wren lived during the building of St Paul's Cathedral. Next is the Globe Theatre, lovingly reconstructed to be as close as possible to the original venue in which William Shakespeare (1564–1616) was a shareholder and actor.

The stretch just before Southwark Bridge by the Anchor pub, was once called Bear Gardens, recalling its bear-baiting past. Before going up the steps to cross Southwark Bridge to the opposite side of the river, it is worth looking in the pedestrian tunnel beneath the bridge to see the evocative engraving that recalls the frost fairs that were held on the tidal Thames. The building of the medieval

Opposite: *Look back across the river for a striking contrast between the sturdy cast-iron spans of the 1921 Southwark bridge and the 95-storey, aptly named 'Shard' beyond, with 11,000 exterior glass panels providing the glitter.*

London Bridge slowed down the river's flow because of its narrow arches. The slowness of the river meant that in severe winters the Thames froze over completely, and in 1564 the first frost fair was held, complete with roasting oxen and entertainments. The fairs came to an end in 1814 when a new London Bridge, the next downstream crossing, was built with broader spans to allow a stronger tide flow. A toll bridge was opened at Southwark in 1819, but people preferred to go downstream to cross at toll-free London Bridge. The bridge here today opened in 1921, true to the style of John Rennie the Elder's original cast-iron structure. After crossing Southwark Bridge, turn left down steps by Vintner's Court to Three Barrels Walk.

Queenhithe and the Fleet

Pass beneath imposing columns fronting Vintner's Court and turn right at the cobbled path bordering the big inlet of Queenhithe for a brief section along the road. Shipwrights during Saxon times operated around the inlet of Queenhithe, until the low medieval London Bridge, built in AD 1000, forced them to move downsteam of it; only shallow-hulled vessels could now berth upstream of the bridge. Together with Billingsgate (see pages 100–10, *Wharves and Warehouses* walk), this was the site of one of London's oldest docks. Some say Queenhithe is named after Matilda, the queen of Henry I (1068–1135); others say that it is derived from the place's early use as a landing place for corn – from the word 'quern', meaning a corn-grinding mill. As you can glean from the local street names, the dock later handled wine. During the 1666 Great Fire of London, Queenhithe was a ferry crossing point for fleeing citizens; many of their valuables, which fell into the river at the time, have since been recovered; the mud contains minimal oxygen, which makes it an excellent preservative against tarnish and decay. However, digging along any of the Thames shore either here or between the Tower of London and the Houses of Parliament, is now prohibited unless you are a member of the Society of Mudlarks, an association that works in conjunction with the Museum of London.

Turn left at the road, past Stew Lane, along High Timber Street until the signposted left turn back to the Thames Path at Broken Wharf. From here, the route is straightforward, as the Thames Path has opened this stretch to pedestrians. You pass under the Millennium Bridge opposite the Tate Modern on Bankside, where there is a polar sundial presented by London's tylers and bricklayers to mark the millennium and a row of seats backed by trellised arches, and follow the path to the Blackfriars bridges. The northernmost arch of the road bridge is the closest you will get to the Fleet, London's most famous 'lost' river, which was mostly channelled into underground pipes and channels in the mid-18th century. The Anglo-Saxon word 'fleet' referred to a navigable river, but that was long ago; a Roman barge with a cargo of stone was found buried in the mud near the mouth of the river in 1962 and is now in the Museum of London.

Ancient History

You are now leaving the outer limits of the Roman port of Londinium – which was delineated by the 600-foot (180-m) mouth of the Fleet River and the city wall that reached the Thames at Ludgate – approaching the Saxon port of Lundenwic. The Anglo-Saxons, whose tribes had overrun post-Roman Britain, began their new port in AD 600, on land that stretched between what now lies below Covent Garden and the Strand. At that time, the river spread to where the Strand (meaning beach) runs today and was rich with eels, salmon, roach, pike, mussels and oysters. There were no quays or warehouses; business was done boat-to-shore – the Anglo-Saxon word 'wic', as in Lundenwic, meant market. Goods from settlements throughout Northern Europe were unloaded from Saxon ships, which took on woven cloth for their return journey.

As prosperity increased in the 7th and 8th centuries, Lundenwic attracted the attention of land-hungry Vikings, who attacked during the 9th century. The new timber London Bridge, which the Saxons built in AD 1000, limited passage upstream to those vessels that could pass beneath it at low tide and was as much a defence against Viking invaders as a means of crossing the river. Alfred the Great (849–99) drove out the Vikings in 886, but 100 years later they were back. In some ways the Viking impact on Britain was beneficial, as they were intrepid explorers who had sailed deep into Europe and crossed the Atlantic to North America. They did much to boost London's trade and introduce new cargoes.

Continue along the river beyond the Blackfriars road bridge. On the opposite side of the road, the elegant Gothic red-brick building on the right after the Art Deco Unilever Building is Sion Hall, which houses an ecclesiastical library; the building dates from 1886. On the river is HMS *President*, a First World War escort ship. Enjoy the decorative cast-iron work on the route: the dolphins on the lamp posts and the benches whose arm-rest motif changes from camels, within the City of London precincts, to sphinxes. Look out for the armorial dragons on either side of the road, which mark the western boundary of the City of London. The area of gardens and buildings on the right is Temple, named for the Knights Templar, founded to guard the Church of the Holy Sepulchre in Jerusalem, who were based here. The order was suppressed by the Pope in 1312 and lawyers moved in. Temple is now one of London's Inns of Court, so-called because in medieval times the buildings were hostelries for barristers and students.

A line of trees at Inner and Middle Temple marks the point where the Great Fire reached in 1666. At the corner of Temple Place, just after Temple Underground Station, is a statue of the Victorian engineer Isambard Kingdom

Brunel. On the river, HQS *Wellington* served in the Second World War, but is now used as a livery hall for the Company of Master Mariners.

Bazalguette Strikes Again

The Palladian-style 800-foot (243-m) terrace of Somerset House up on the right just before Waterloo Bridge, is the result of an 18th-century uplift, but the building takes its name from Lord Protector Somerset, who built a house on the site in 1547. The arched recesses in its basement were once watergates, which controlled the flow of water at high tide.

Beyond Waterloo Bridge, the stretch lying ahead of you is Sir Joseph Bazalguette's Victoria Embankment: there's a memorial to him at the far end, just after Charing Cross and Hungerford bridges. Balzalguette's embankment wall was built 14 feet (4.3m) below low-water mark and 20 feet (6m) above high-water mark; laid-out gardens and courtyards were created above the course of the underground. In the 17th and 18th centuries, elegant aristocratic residences, interspersed with coal and timber wharves, lined the shore and the river lapped against the Duke of Buckingham's gardens at York House. The York Watergate, in Victoria Embankment Gardens, led from the duke's garden to the river stairs.

But first you pass, rising above the gardens on the right, the late 19th-century Savoy Hotel, commissioned by Richard D'Oyly Carte (1844–1901), manager of the Gilbert and Sullivan 'Savoy' operettas. There's a memorial to W. S. Gilbert opposite Embankment Station. The Savoy's cream terracotta tiles were made at the Doulton factory, which then sat across the river in Lambeth. On the left is Cleopatra's Needle, an Egyptian obelisk which dates back to *c.*1475 BC. It has no known historical connection with Cleopatra, who it in fact predates by about 1,400 years. The obelisk was encased in a specially constructed cylindrical pontoon to tow it from Africa, and, after being accidentally dropped in and retrieved from the Bay of Biscay, eventually arrived in England in 1878.

Continue past Embankment Station and the Balzalguette memorial. Across the road is a bust of Samuel Plimsoll (1824–98) erected by the Seamen's Union 'for his services to men of the sea of all nations'. Plimsoll was responsible for making ships much safer for those who sailed in them, not least by his invention of the Plimsoll line, which indicated safe cargo levels. After the RAF memorial, with its golden eagle, a bronze bas-relief continues the RAF theme, in a memorial to the airmen who fought the 1940 German air attack known as 'The Battle of Britain'. Continue to Westminster Bridge and turn right to the underground station.

SPORTING THAMES: PUTNEY–CHISWICK– BARNES–PUTNEY

Summary: We take a break from the hard-working Thames and escape to Putney and beyond, following in the footsteps of Charles II (1630–85) and Nell Gwynn (1650–87), of Victorian Londoners on day trips by train and of wealthy merchants from the port of London looking for out-of-town riverside properties. This is the recreational Thames, for messing about on or beside; a river that is uncluttered by too many bridges, traffic or industry. We dip into rowing and yachting, follow part of the University Boat Race course and experience the impact of the sea on this section of upper tideway. The walk can easily be split into two at Barnes or, if you want a full day out, aim for a pub lunch at Chiswick and digest it on the return journey.

START AND FINISH:	Putney Bridge Underground Station
DISTANCE:	7 miles (11.7km)
REFRESHMENTS:	Putney High Street and riverside; Chiswick waterfront; Hammersmith riverfront pubs; Barnes waterfront and village.

The Impact of the Railways

From Putney Bridge Station, turn left and cross the road (Ranelagh Gardens) to a path alongside the railway bridge (signed Thames Path) and turn right at the river. In the 1930s, the railways introduced day excursions at a price that ordinary people could afford. The riverside villages and farmland just outside London became accessible and many boatyards operating pleasure boats opened upstream from Westminster to serve the new customers. It wasn't until the 1880s that the railway reached Putney and, though we cannot see it today, a footpath led from the station platform to a new pier where pleasure steamers awaited.

Follow the path to the right, past a pavement mosaic dedicated to the Oxford & Cambridge University Boat Race, and over Swan Drawdock with its wild water garden at the far (inland) end. Boats drew in the dock at high water and unloaded cargo on to carts on the shore at low tide. Continue along the river to a willow tree and turn right across a paved area, then left to go through the foot

The Dove PH   *Furnival Gardens*

Old Ship PH

GREAT WEST ROAD

Walpole House

UPPER MALL   *Lower*
Mall

Linden   Hammersmith Pier
House

Blue Anchor PH

Hammersmith
Terrace

HAMMERSMITH BRIDGE

CHISWICK LANE SOUTH

MAWSON LANE

GREAT WEST ROAD

CHISWICK MALL

HOGARTH LANE

Chiswick
Eyot

LONSDALE ROAD

Harrods'
Depository

BURLINGTON
LANE

CHURCH ST

FISHERMAN'S
PLACE

CHISWICK
WHARF

St Nicholas's Church

Corney Reach

LONSDALE ROAD

Nature
Reserve

N

London
Wetland
Centre

500m (549 yards)

THE PROMENADE

River Thames

LONSDALE ROAD

Duke's
Meadows

Barnes
Bridge

BARNES ST

THE TERRACE

Barnes Bridge
Railway Station

tunnel beneath the road bridge. This bridge dates from 1884, but its wooden predecessor of 1729 was the first to cross the Thames between London Bridge and Kingston. Putney enjoyed its exclusive crossing point for another 20 years, before Westminster (1750), Blackfriars (1769) and Battersea (1773) bridges were built downstream. Putney Bridge became a watershed between the working and

Hammersmith Underground Station

HAMMERSMITH FLYOVER

CRISP RD

CHANCELLOR'S RD

FULHAM PALACE ROAD

Riverside Studios

WINSLOW RD

WINDSOR RD

PARFREY ST

COLWITH RD

RAINVILLE ROAD

River Café

Richard Rogers' Architects

Crabtree Dock

QUEENSMILL RD

WOODLAWN RD

STEVENAGE ROAD

River Thames

Fulham Football Ground

STEVENAGE RD

Beverley Brook

EMBANKMENT

BISHOPS AVE

BISHOPS PARK RD

FULHAM PALACE ROAD

FULHAM ROAD

FULHAM HIGH STREET

NEW KINGS ROAD

Bishop's Park

Fulham Palace

Thames Path

Putney Bridge Underground Station

RANELAGH GARDENS

Thames Rowing Club
Ranelagh Yacht Club
Vesta Rowing Club
London Rowing Club

RISHMOND ROAD

EMBANKMENT

Putney Pier

PUTNEY HIGH STREET

PUTNEY BRIDGE

Swan Drawdock

leisure-orientated Thames. There was already a long-established upriver boating tradition: Charles II, a pioneer of yachting as a recreational sport, reserved several of his fleet for 'up-river' sailing and, as we shall see later on the walk, he visited local hostelries with his mistress, Nell Gwynn. In the late 19th century, when the river downstream of Putney was becoming congested and the many bridges hindered navigation, small boat-hire yards and boating clubs either foundered or moved upstream. The University Boat Race relocated from its original Westminster–Putney course to its present Putney–Mortlake stretch in 1845.

Views of Putney

The foot tunnel opens into Bishop's Park, so called because it encompasses the grounds of Fulham Palace, which used to be the official residence of the bishops of London until their move to Westminster in 1973. In the 16th century it had a botanical garden with many hitherto unknown exotic plants. The Tudor palace is still there, though you cannot see it from the riverside walk.

Turn left through the park; the church here and riverside promenade were the sites of a famous scene in the cult horror film *The Omen*, starring Gregory Peck. Look over the river to Putney Pier; the starting point of the University Boat Race is just downstream of it. The path is an excellent and popular vantage point for the start of the race, which is held in March. A little further along, as you pass beneath the mottled branches of mature London plane trees, look across to see a line of rowing-club boathouses, which you will pass at the end of the walk.

Continue along the path until you have no option but to turn right at the boundary of Fulham Football Ground, owned by Mohammed Al-Fayed, and the only English league football club to exhibit a Grade 1 listed building, 'The Cottage'. Leave the park and turn left along Stevenage Road. At the end of the red-brick façade, turn sharp left along a narrow path bordered by a small park and rejoin the river. After you have passed a tiered apartment block opposite a terrace of yellow-brick houses with tiny gardens, look across the river to see a sculpture of two flying swans and then to where a small obelisk commands an opening in the bankside vegetation. This, which we will look at more closely on the return journey, marks the first mile of the Boat Race's 4 miles and 374 yards (7km).

Richard Rogers' Territory

Our upstream route turns north, as the river's course heads south, along the downstream side of an enormous meander. The path is punctuated by grassy patches – meadows and orchards back in the 17th century – which now provide exhibition space for the occasional rusting sculptures made from machine parts. The river bank is almost obscured in summer by buddleia. By now, the sultry green folly of Hammersmith Bridge can be seen in the distance, but we are about to leave the riverside for a spell. The path narrows; go up a flight of steps to look along a stretch of river that was once crowded with wharves where market-garden produce was loaded on to barges and taken to feed the London population. The path heads inland just before a flight of steps, passing to the right of the Crab Tree pub, which is on the site of the former Crabtree Dock boatyard. Turn left to go past the pub and left again beyond the 1907 Palace Wharf warehouse to return to the riverside path. A modern building of blue, green and glass with an arched roof was, until 2015, the base of Richard Rogers' architectural practice. The practice moved to another of its landmark buildings, the Leadenhall Building (also known as 'The Cheesegrater') in the City. The River Café, designed by Rogers and co-founded by his wife Ruth, and Rose Gray, in the next building are still up-and-running. Look across the river to where the bulk of Harrods' Depository dominates this stretch of river. The furniture storage house was built in 1894 on the site of market gardens that grew produce for

Opposite: *Hammersmith suspension bridge, with its magnificent piers, was designed by Sir Joseph Bazalguette, the Victorian engineer responsible for the Embankment and sorting out London's sewage systems. Coxswains in the University Boat Race teams use a particular lamp post as a sight line for the deepest part of the river – and the fastest course on which to guide their crews.*

the London markets. Its design echoes that of its parent store in Knightsbridge, central London.

Continue along the path, following a brief diversion inland due to a new residential development, noting a plaque to the engineer/architect of the original Hammersmith Bridge, William Tierney Clark. Just beyond is the gleaming steel *Figurehead* statue by Rick Kirby. There may be temporary diversions around ongoing development as you approach Riverside Studios, which were founded by the British actor Jack Buchanan (1891-1957), but plans do incorporate a continuation of the riverside path.

Bazalguette's Bridge

Hammersmith Bridge is an important landmark for those watching the University Boat Race on television – as it is for the coxes – but it is closed to pedestrians during the race. This was not always the case: in 1870 there were more than 11,000 spectators on the bridge, causing great concern as the structure was already deemed too weak for its weight of road traffic. The great Victorian engineer Sir Joseph Bazalguette designed the present bridge, which opened in 1887. He made the most of the decorative potential of cast iron, then a relatively new building material, making latticework railings, towers topped with French château-style roofs and armorial decorative features. The original bridge, which opened in 1827, was less elaborate but was the first suspension bridge across the Thames. Local resident William Tierney Clarke was the engineer; there's an image of his design on his tomb in the parish church, and it's the subject of engravings found in many a local pub.

Beyond Hammersmith Bridge, round the peak of the loop in the river and then head south along Lower Mall, which is graced by elegant 18th-century houses. If your timing is right, this is a good spot to stop for lunch, for there are a couple of pubs, including the Blue Anchor, which first opened in 1720, and the Dove, a little way farther on. Reach Furnival Gardens, named for Dr Fred Furnival, co-creator of the original *Oxford English Dictionary*, philanthropist, and rowing enthusiast who founded a local sculling club. Hammersmith Pier, with its cluster of barges and houseboats, is near the site of a creek, the tidal mouth of the Stamford Brook, around which the village of Hammersmith grew up. As the name 'Hammersmith' suggests, there was a tradition of iron foundries and forges here, but there were also, in Victorian times, two big breweries, market gardens and brick fields. At the end of the gardens, turn right and then immediately left down a flagstoned alley by the 17th-century Dove pub. Just before the pub is the home of the Doves Press and bookbindery, founded jointly by late Victorian style guru William Morris, Thomas Cobden-Sanderson (the man who coined the 'arts and crafts' description of Morris's style revolution) and local print expert Sir Emery Walker. The pub is featured as 'The Pigeons' in a novel called *The Water Gipsies* by politician and humorist A.P. Herbert (1890–1971), who also lived nearby. Charles II and his mistress Nell Gwynn cavorted there and the poet James Thomson (1700–1748) wrote the words of the rousing *Rule Britannia* in a room upstairs.

Illustrious Residents

The tall, red-brick house with five window bays on the right as you return to the riverside path, was the home of William Morris (see pages 111–17, *The Working Wandle* walk) and is where he died. At the end of this stretch of Upper Mall, Linden House – headquarters of the London Corinthian Sailing Club – is set back from the riverside. The crow's-nest structure on a post opposite is the starting box for club races. This broad reach of the river, open to the prevailing south-westerly winds, is considered to be one of the best for sailing on the tidal Thames. Just on the right, after walking beneath the balconies of some apartments, is the Old Ship pub, which dates from the 16th century but was largely rebuilt in the early 19th century. Then there's another patch of public garden, spliced by a white-arcaded wall, which is all that remains of the West Middlesex Water Company pumping station which used to occupy this land. Turn inland here, with the Black Lion pub ahead, and left into Hammersmith Terrace, home of many an illustrious resident, including Sir Emery Walker (1851–1933) and calligrapher Edward Johnston (1872–1944), designer of a celebrated typeface for London Transport.

Soon you are back on the riverside path again at Chiswick Mall, where the 17th- and 18th-century houses are separated from their riverfront gardens by the road. Famous former residents include Barbara Villiers, Countess of Castlemaine, another favourite mistress of Charles II, who lived in Walpole House (dating from between the 16th and 18th centuries). Opposite, at the same level as the road, is Chiswick Eyot, an island with a crop of pollarded willows. You become aware of the encroaching river at high tide: sometimes the next section of the walk is under a foot or so of water, and you may have to make a detour by turning right down Chiswick Lane South, then left and left again to rejoin the path by St Nicholas's Church. Many of the houses have flood defences, such as heavy iron gates or fences backed with plastic casing, a graphic reminder that we are still – downstream of Teddington Lock – subject to the force of the tidal Thames. Twice a day the sea's tides push the river back towards its source and swell its volume; if the river appears to be flowing in the direction in which we are walking – upstream – the tide is 'making', or coming in. Embankments (see pages 151–60, *Bridging the Thames* walk) built downstream aggravated flooding upstream by narrowing the river and increasing its depth: the Thames at Putney is now 9 feet (3m) deeper than it was 300 years ago.

Boat Race Tactics

Here at Corney Reach we are about 3 miles (5km) into the Boat Race course, and racing crews vie for dominance at the part of the stream where the tide flows strongest. As the loop straightens out, the river is exposed to the full force of the prevailing south-westerly winds and if there's a 'wind-over-tide' situation – with the tide going one way and the wind the other – the resulting waves can sink a shallow racing craft. The 'shape', volume and flow of the water change dramatically between high and low tide and the force of the tide is enormous. A wise cox will spend some time talking to local watermen to check the mood of the river, for the course he or she will steer to take advantage of tidal flow is a vital element in racing.

At the end of Chiswick Mall, where the church of St Nicholas, patron saint of sailors, is on the right, turn left to return to the riverside path. The church is the burial place of Barbara Villiers, mistress of Charles II, and of artists William Hogarth (1697–1764) and James McNeill Whistler (1834–1903). Continue past residential developments at Corney Reach until the formal path ends abruptly and enters a field. Triangular ceramic sculptures mark the beginning of Duke's Meadows and you can choose from two or three levels of path, initially bordered by poplars. Continue past an abandoned pavilion, a slipway and a boathouse (from which there are good views over to Barnes riverside) to steps leading up to Barnes Bridge, which you cross.

The three-arched, cast-iron railway bridge was opened in 1849 and, although the footbridge attachment was made especially strong to support Boat Race crowds, it

Shoveler

is actually closed for the race. If you are watching from the bank, you cannot see the finish, which is a short way beyond the next bridge (Chiswick). However, the winner is usually (though by no means always) decided by this point. The crews race against the stream but with the incoming tidal flow, which is about one hour before high water at Putney.

An Oarsman's Paradise

After descending the railway-bridge steps, cross the road and turn right along the footpath beside the road, before veering left down the gravel path to the riverside. Now you can relax from history and architecture, with maybe just the occasional recap as you glimpse places you have passed on the other side of the river, and enjoy a pleasant stroll through a tunnel of trees occasionally interrupted by riverside homes. Inland is the award-winning London Wetland Centre; it is not accessible from the river, but worth a visit to see protected wetland species from all over the world.

You will know when you are a mile or so from Putney Bridge, because you pass the memorial to oarsman and rowing coach Steve Fairbairn, who founded another classic rowing event – the Head of the River Race. There's a footbridge across one of suburban London's surviving rivers, the Beverley Brook, whose course can be followed intermittently to Wimbledon Common and Richmond Park.

The path opens up to a waterfront road flanked by boat clubs: Thames Rowing Club is recognized as one of the world's leading rowing clubs for women, who make up 60 per cent of the membership, and was founded in 1860. Ranelagh Yacht Club, also founded in the mid-19th century, took its name from an 18th-century sailing race from Westminster to Putney Bridge; both the club and the race were forced to move upstream to their present location by 19th-century bridge-building. Vesta is the third oldest rowing club on this stretch, after London and Thames, and is, they say, named after the first tug that sailed past after the club's foundation (the tug, in turn, was named after music-hall star Vesta Tilley). The oldest rowing club is the last we pass: London Rowing Club (LRC) was founded in 1856, although the present balconied clubhouse dates from 1870. Former LRC member and celebrated racing driver Graham Hill and his son Damon wore the dark blue and white club colours on their racing helmets. Traditionally, the LRC was a men-only club, but the first female rowing members were accepted in 2002.

At Boat Race time you may wish to do this walk in reverse in order to catch some of the race. But, unless you can maintain a 15mph (20kmph) sprint to keep up with the crews, you'd better set off early in order to reach a vantage point near the finish at Barnes Bridge or just beyond. To return to Putney Bridge Underground Station, follow the road to the bridge and turn left to cross it.

THAMES-SIDE RETREATS: KEW–RICHMOND

Summary: This walk celebrates the elegant homes and gardens that the Thames-side position has inspired between Kew and Richmond. The upper tidal Thames leaves industry in its place, downstream. Royal palaces were built along this route from medieval times, particularly from the Tudor period. The royals brought with them the most fashionable artists and architects to embellish their country retreats and in their wake came wealthy retainers and merchants enriched by Port of London trade.

START:	Kew Bridge Railway Station or Kew Gardens Underground and Railway Station
FINISH:	Richmond Underground and Railway Station
DISTANCE:	6 miles (10km)
REFRESHMENTS:	Kew Gardens Station area; Kew Green; Richmond riverside

If you are starting from Kew Bridge Railway Station, turn right and at the traffic lights cross to Kew Bridge and join the riverside path to go upstream (right) towards Richmond – a 10-minute walk at the most. Alternatively, it takes about 15 minutes to reach the river from Kew Gardens Underground and Railway Station: cross the area in front of the station obliquely right to head down Station Approach. Turn right at the end down Leyborne Park (the alley which runs parallel is rather dark and grubby). Turn left at busy Mortlake Road and, at the traffic lights, cross Kew Road to Kew Green. Cross the Green on the path that goes obliquely behind St Anne's Church, which was built with the help of a £100 donation from Queen Anne in the early 18th century. The slab of gravestone surrounded by railings on the south side of the church is where the 18th-century court painter Thomas Gainsborough (1727–88) is buried.

The elegant Georgian houses round the Green date mainly from the late 18th century, built for courtiers and officials who served King George III's (1738–1820) summer residence at Kew. There have been royal palaces in Kew and Richmond since medieval times, and the Royal Botanic Gardens evolved

Kew Bridge Railway Station

KEW BRIDGE ROAD

KEW BRIDGE

KEW ROAD

Brentford Ait

FERRY LANE

Lots Ait

Kew Green

St Anne's Church

River Brent

Brentford

Kew Palace

Kew Gardens

KEW GARDENS RD

Royal Botanic Gardens

Syon House

Kew Gardens Underground and Railway Station

STATION APPROACH

MORTLAKE ROAD

Syon Park

Syon Reach

Old Isleworth

Isleworth Ait

Old Deer Park

RICHMOND RD

King's Observatory

River Crane

ST MARGARET'S RD

KEW ROAD

LOWER MORTLAKE RD

Richmond Green

TWICKENHAM ROAD

THE QUADRANT

Richmond Underground & Railway Station

Richmond Lock

Asgill House

Richmond

FRIARS LA

THE GREEN

GEORGE ST

SHEEN RD

TWICKENHAM BRIDGE

Cholmondeley Walk

BREWERS LANE

WATER LANE

HILL ST

O'Higgins Square

RICHMOND BRIDGE

PETERSHAM ROAD

RICHMOND HILL

Terrace Gardens

Terrace Field

QUEEN'S RD

N

Richmond Park

500m (549 yards)

Twickenham

Petersham Meadows

from the gardens that were laid out around the palaces; the main entrance to Kew Gardens is to the left of the Green.

The Making of Kew

The future Queen Caroline, wife of George II (1683–1760), set the ball rolling by hiring William Kent (c.1685–1748) and Charles Bridgeman (d. 1738) – both pioneers in the golden age of naturalistic landscape gardening – to lay out the grounds of Richmond Lodge in the Old Deer Park, which we pass later. At the time of Caroline's death, in 1737, the gardens reached as far as today's Kew. But it was her son Frederick and his wife Augusta who were responsible for creating the first Kew Gardens around their (since demolished) palace. After Frederick's death, Augusta, with the help of architects and horticulturalists, began collecting rare and exotic plants. Some of the trees planted at that time are still living, including the first pagoda and ginkgo trees introduced to England, and the Orangery and Pagoda (the structure as opposed to the tree) are surviving buildings. The next king, George III, built on Augusta's work and, with the naturalist Sir Joseph Banks (1743–1820), consolidated Kew's place as a superlative collection of plants from around the world, and opened the gardens to the public.

Cross from the Green to Ferry Lane, which once led to the Brentford ferry that carried horses, carriages and people across the river from the mid-17th century until the 20th century. Turn left along the river bank (signed Kew Gardens), via the towpath. Just downstream, the first Kew Bridge was built in the 1750s, though the present bridge dates from 1903.

Across the river is Brentford (see pages 20–27, *A Flight of Locks* walk) and an island called Brentford Ait that is lush in high summer with oak, willow and poplar trees in full leaf. Between the 14th and 18th centuries, osier willows for basket-making were cultivated on the island. The word 'ait' is a corruption of the Anglo-Saxon *eyot* (islet). There are several aits along the river, formed from silts and gravels washed down by tributary rivers. The next is Lots Ait and shortly afterwards you can see where the River Brent meets the Thames.

In the 18th century, the elegance of Brentford almost matched that of Kew and Richmond. In the 19th century, however, the outlet you see across the river was a busy dock, where the Grand Junction (later Grand Union) Canal joined the Thames, and was later the terminus of a branch line of Isambard Kingdom Brunel's Great Western Railway. Instead of the smart marina and waterside development there today, you would have seen concentrated activity: barges lined up along the

Opposite: *Look across the river to Syon Park, home of the Dukes of Somerset and Northumberland at key moments in history, and the grandest piece of real estate on this stretch of the Thames. The green-domed pavilion was built as a boathouse when Syon House was remodeled by architect Robert Adam in the second half of the 18th century.*

wharves, some laden with coal and lime and others ready to take produce from market gardens or hay for the working horses of London. From the mid-19th century until the dock's closure in the 1960s, the scene was packed with warehouses and railway freight yards.

Syon Park and the Old Deer Park

Meanwhile, on the left, you can gain some idea of the extent of Princess Augusta's Kew Gardens as you walk along their western boundary. Individual features are hidden by bank and trees until, towards the end, you look over an area of wild meadow planting. The vista over the river opens up at Syon Park, our next palatial Thames-side residence. This one has been the home of the Percy family, earls of Northumberland, since 1594. The lion above the clock tower was transported by barge along the Thames from a Northumberland family home in the Strand. The name is taken from Sion Hill in Palestine and the house, of which the original Tudor shell remains, was built on the site of a medieval convent. In the second half of the 18th century, the house and grounds had a complete makeover by another couple of style giants of the period: architect-designer Robert Adam (1728–92) and landscape gardener Lancelot 'Capability' Brown (1715–83). The tidal meadow, so called because the river floods over it twice daily at high tide – a rarity for the crowded banks of the Thames – has been designated a Site of Special Scientific Interest.

The whole of the Thames along this stretch is an inviting corridor for wildlife, with freshwater habitats now taking over from the salt-marsh that dominates further downstream. The sea tide reaches as far as Teddington Lock further upstream, but its salty influence is more diluted here. Soon you'll see a pink and white confection of a building on the riverside, which is the very splendid Pavilion built to the design of Robert Mylne in 1803. It originally adjoined the boathouse where the Duke of Northumberland's state barge, which was probably used for entertaining, was kept.

The path is now raised above the main river and an overflow channel. Excavated earth built up the path, which doubled as a dyke against river flood water. The way runs through a tunnel of trees alongside Syon Reach; keep your eyes on the alert above for some splendid specimens of beefsteak fungus. Soon, about an hour into the walk, there's a break in the trees, overlooking a pond rich in flowers and hunted by red darter dragonflies in summer, and a view that opens out across the Old Deer Park, royal hunting grounds of 700 years ago. This is where Richmond Lodge was sited, official residence of the future King George II and Queen Caroline when Caroline started her gardening plans. Look between the twin steel obelisks along the meridian line by which the king's time was set before Greenwich took over this role in 1884. The Observatory itself was commissioned by George III, who wanted the best chance of watching the transit of the star Venus in 1769. Today, the Old Deer Park is owned by the Crown Estate and is open to the public.

Old Isleworth to Richmond

Now, on the opposite bank, we are passing what could almost pass for a rural English village, but is in fact Old Isleworth. There's a sign advertising the Isleworth ferry, which operates at weekends from May to September. In the 19th century the village was surrounded by market gardens producing strawberries, raspberries and other fruit for London markets. Knowing how the islets of the Thames form, it is no surprise that just upstream of Isleworth Ait is the outlet of the River Crane, from which, in the Middle Ages, a channel was cut to power the corn mill at Syon Abbey. The little hamlet of Twickenham, now a widespread suburban area on the far bank, grew up in the fork of land between the Thames and the Crane. The peace of this wooded stretch may be broken by the shrieks of green parakeets. You may hear the tapping of adult birds pecking through the bark of the trees to create woodpecker-style nests. Although an invasive species, which has colonized many of south-west London's parks, local ornithologists claim that the birds do not threaten the native indigenous wildlife.

Continue to Richmond Lock, which was completed in 1894 and the last lock on the downstream course of the Thames. Take a brief detour up to the footbridge to look down at the great chambers and gates. The lock and weir were designed to increase the river's depth and flow to prevent the build-up of silt and sewage; this was becoming such a serious problem in the late 19th century that pleasure boats would run aground and the river was reduced to a noisome trickle. So much water was being extracted to meet the enormous demands of the downstream metropolis, said the engineers, that the river's upstream flow couldn't carry it. Not only did it have to cope with local sewage, but also that which was swept upstream from London on the incoming tide.

A few yards after the lock, you pass beneath the concrete arches and bronze balustrades of Twickenham Bridge (1933) and another bridge that carried the railway to Richmond from 1846. You are now on the outskirts of Richmond. On the left is Asgill House (1758), home of wealthy City banker and one-time mayor of London, Sir Charles Asgill. When Sir Charles threw a party for his City associates, guests were ferried upriver in barges with on-board bands. Pleasure, and even ceremonial, barges must often have added glamour to this stretch of the Thames as the rich and royal made their visits. Prince Frederick (of Kew Gardens fame) was also a great party host of the 18th century, bringing in orchestras, theatricals and masquerades. He loved the river and was a great supporter of rowing races. He commissioned his house architect William Kent

Beefsteak fungus

to design a state barge, which he used for musical concerts as well as for ferrying his family along the river.

One of the most magnificent and poignant sights, however, must have been that of Queen Elizabeth I on her last voyage from Richmond Palace by barge as the poet William Camden described: 'The Queen was brought by water to Whitehall/At every stroke the oars did tears fall'. Continue along Cholmondeley Walk, with its eminently stylish bow-windowed Georgian residences and, when you cross Water Lane – which you may have to negotiate at high tide – you will have arrived in riverside café land and the broad, stepped terraces beneath a modern Neo-classical-style development.

Into the Heart of Richmond

Continue beside the river, past the boat-building sheds and under Richmond Bridge. The soft grey Purbeck stone lines of the original 1777 structure were cleverly preserved when the bridge had to be widened in 1939. Your distance from London Bridge is now 11¹/₄ miles (18.8km) by river, while upstream, 15 river miles away, is Windsor. Immediately after the bridge pass beneath O'Higgins Square, named after General Bernardo O'Higgins (*c.*1778–1842), Chilean statesman (of Irish extraction) and liberator of his country from the Spanish, who studied in Richmond for three years from 1795. After five minutes or so, you will pass Richmond canoe clubs on the left just before a large white building, a former pub. Here, strike up through the gardens left away from the river and cross Petersham Road into Terrace Gardens. Follow the paths up and right through the gardens, noting the coade-stone statue of the River God Thames, which was the single most expensive item in the 'Coadestone Catalogue of Architectural Statuary and Ornament' of 1784.

The reason for this detour away from the river becomes obvious as soon as you emerge from the gardens in the top right-hand corner. Here, from a gravelled terrace on Richmond Hill, high above the river, is a view that has inspired many an artist and writer, including J.M.W. Turner, Charles Dickens, Sir Walter Scott (1771–1832) and Robert Bridges (1844–1930). You can read excerpts from their poems and identify points of view with the help of information panels. The houses above the terrace are highly sought after, while immediately below are the Petersham Meadows where horses and cows still graze.

Cut down a path that goes straight through Terrace Field just beyond the information panels. Cross Petersham Road again and turn right along the riverside path. Head back towards Richmond Bridge, past the largest plane tree in Greater London, under the bridge and across Water Lane. Take Friars Lane, the next turning right, and cross Richmond Green, with its elegant border of Queen Anne and Georgian houses, obliquely right. The Green was once the scene of jousting tournaments. Turn right through Brewers Lane into George Street and head left uphill until you see Richmond Underground and Railway Station on your right.

GAZETTEER

This gazetteer gives, in chapter order, the website addresses of places to visit mentioned in the book. Check online for locations, opening times, prices and more.

HAY AND BRICKS

Perivale Wood Nature Reserve, www.perivalewood.k-hosting.co.uk

A FLIGHT OF LOCKS

Boston Manor, www.hounslow.info/arts-culture/historic-houses-museums/boston-manor-house

Kew Bridge Steam Museum, Osterley Park, www.nationaltrust.org.uk/osterley-park/?p=1356312744250

SHORT CUTS TO LIMEHOUSE

Mile End Park, www.towerhamlets.gov.uk/lgsl/451-500/461_parks/mile_end_park.aspx

Ragged School Museum, www.raggedschoolmuseum.org.uk

BARGES GO WEST

Camden Lock Markets, www.camdenlock.net

Canal Museum, www.canalmuseum.org.uk

Victoria Park, www.towerhamlets.gov.uk/default.aspx?page=12670

REGENCY WATERWAY

Camley Street Natural Park, www.wildlondon.org.uk/reserves/camley-street-natural-park

The Pirate Castle, www.thepiratecastle.org

London Zoo, www.zsl.org/zsl-london-zoo

GEORGIAN DOCK BOOM

Museum of London Docklands, www.museumoflondon.org.uk/docklands

GEORGIAN DOCKS REVISITED

Thames Police Museum (by appointment only), www.thames-policemuseum.org.uk/museum.html

BULK CARGO

Mudchute City Farm, www.mudchute.org

Isle of Dogs archives, www.islandhistory.org.uk

ROYAL FAVOURITES

For National Maritime Museum, The Queen's House, Royal Observatory, Peter Harrison Planetarium, and Cutty Sark, www.rmg.co.uk

Royal Naval College, www.ornc.org

SURREY SIDE UP

Brunel Museum, www.brunel-museum.org.uk

Midnight Apothecary Garden, www.facebook.com/Midnight Apothecary

Pumphouse Educational Museum, www.culture24.org.uk/am10804

REINVENTING THE LANDSCAPE

Events, www.greenwichpeninsula.co.uk/on-the-peninsula

Greenwich Ecology Park, www.greenwichecologypark.com

O2 Arena, www.theo2.co.uk

Thames Barrier, www.royalgreenwich.gov.uk/info/200043/extra-curricular_activities/160/thames_barrier_information_and_learning_centre

WHARVES AND WAREHOUSES

City Hall, www.london.gov.uk/city-hall

Design Museum, www.designmuseum.org

Golden Hinde, www.goldenhinde.com

HMS Belfast, www.iwm.org.uk/visits/hms-belfast

Southwark Cathedral, *http:// cathedral.southwark.anglican.org*

Tower Bridge, *www.towerbridge.org.uk*

Tower of London, *www.hrp.org.uk/TowerOfLondon*

THE WORKING WANDLE
Wandsworth museum collection, Battersea Town Hall, *www.wandsworthmuseum.co.uk*

Merton Abbey Mills, *www.mertonabbeymills.org.uk*

THE COUNTRY WANDLE
Morden Hall, *www.nationaltrust. org.uk/morden-hall-park*

Wandle Industrial Museum, *www.wandle.org/visitingus/visitingus.html*

OLD RIVERS FOR NEW
Queen Elizabeth Park (former Olympic Park), *www.queenelizabetholympicpark.co.uk*

Lea/Lee Valley information, *www.visitleevalley.org.uk*

Three Mills, *www.housemill.org.uk*

BRIDGING THE THAMES
Globe Theatre, *www.shakespearesglobe.com*

Houses of Parliament, *www.parliament.uk/visiting*

Lambeth Palace, *www.archbishop-ofcanterbury.org/pages/visit-lambeth-palace.html*

London Eye, *www.londoneye.com*

Garden Museum, *www.gardenmuseum.org.uk*

Museum of London, *www.museumoflondon.org.uk*

Southbank Centre, *www.southbankcentre.co.uk*

Tate Modern, *www.tate.org.uk/visit/tate-modern*

Westminster Abbey, *www.westminster-abbey.org*

SPORTING THAMES
London Wetland Centre, *www.wwt.org.uk/wetland-centres/london*

THAMES-SIDE RETREATS
Royal Botanic Gardens, *www.kew.org*

Hampton Court, *www.hrp.org.uk/HamptonCourtPalace*

BIBLIOGRAPHY

Pevsner Architectural Guides to London Nikolaus Pevsner (various dates)

London Docklands, An Architectural Guide Elizabeth Williamson & Nikolaus Pevsner (Penguin Books, 1998)

The Times *London History Atlas* ed. H. Clout (Times Books, 1991)

Geology of London and South-east England G.M. Davies (1939)

The Lost Rivers of London Nicholas Barton (Historical Publications, 1992)

London, Biography of a City Christopher Hibbert (Penguin Books, 1980)

Dockland S.K. Al Naib (Thames and Hudson, 1986)

Canals and Waterways Michael E. Ware (Shire Publications Ltd, 1995)

A Guide to London's Riverside Suzanne Ebel and Doreen Impey (Constable, 1985)

London, A Biography Peter Ackroyd (Vintage, 2001)

London and Docklands Walks S.K. Al Naib (University of East London, 2000)

The Green London Way Bob Gilbert (Lawrence & Wishart, 1991)

Time Out *Book of London Walks* ed. Andrew White (Penguin Books, 2001)

Canal Walks: South Ray Quinlan (Sutton Publishing, 1994)

Walks Along the Thames Path Ron Emmons (New Holland, 2001)

Andrew Duncan's Favourite London Walks Andrew Duncan (New Holland, 2002)

Wandsworth Past Dorian Gerhold (Historical Publications, 1998)

Wren's London Eric de Maré (Michael Joseph, 1977)

The National Trust Guide to Our Industrial Past Anthony Burton (Mitchell Beazley, 1983)

WEBSITES

www.britainexpress.com
www.canalrivertrust.org.uk
www.gov.uk/government/organisations/environment-agency
www.greenwich-guide.org.uk
www.islandhistory.org.uk
www.lddc-history.org.uk
http://riverconditions.environment-agency.gov.uk

INDEX

ACKNOWLEDGEMENTS

With special thanks to Chris Elmers at Museum in Docklands, the Canal Museum for help in research, and Nick Fordham, Christopher Grainger, Caroline Hill, Charlotte Louveaux, and my son Garth McWilliam, for checking some of the routes.